The
Easy

Ingredient
Diabetic
Cookbook
The Smart Way
to Cook Healthy

The Easy 4 Ingredient
Diabetic Cookbook

1st Printing   July 2005
2nd Printing   April 2006

ISBN 1-931294-56-9 Hard Cover
Library of Congress Catalog 2005926706

Illustrated by Nancy Murphy Griffith
Typesetting by Fit-To-Print, Dallas, Texas

Manufactured in China
Designed in the United States of America by
Cookbook Resources, LLC
541 Doubletree Drive
Highland Village, Texas 75077
Toll free 866-229-2665
www.cookbookresources.com

cookbook
resources® LLC

From the Author

Caught in the rush of everyday living? Even the most health-conscious consumer would agree that healthy eating and cooking are quite a challenge! After a hard day of work, we hurry to the supermarket, grabbing familiar foods that are quick and easy to prepare, but that are probably not the healthiest food choices.

After the publication of my first book, *Easy Healthy Cooking with Four Ingredients*, I became aware of just how important easy, quick and healthy recipes are. Over and over again, people have said, "Four healthy ingredients? That's what I need!"

When I began researching nutrition requirements for diabetics, it became clear to me that the recommended foods for people with diabetes are essentially the same healthy foods everyone needs. The challenge was to develop recipes using smart, convenient products designed for people on the go, yet still be low in sugar and refined carbohydrates, sodium, fat, cholesterol and calories. Impossible? Never!

Reading food labels and looking for smart new products is a great idea, but it sometimes takes more time than we have. That hungry family waiting at home is the more urgent need, not roaming the aisles of the supermarket. I've done the research for you, providing nearly 200 smart recipes with nutritional analyses, serving sizes – even net carb counts. This cookbook takes all guesswork out of meal planning.

For the person with diabetes, the low carb dieter, or anyone short on time and long on good intentions, this cookbook is for you. *Enjoy!*

Sally N. Hunt, Ph.D. is the author of Easy Healthy Cooking with 4 Ingredients, published by Cookbook Resources, LLC, 2003, which has sold more than 10,000 copies. She has appeared on QVC Home Shopping Network and local television programs. With a Ph.D. in Home Economics, Dr. Hunt has extensive teaching experience at the college level. She is enjoying retirement in historic Natchitoches, Louisiana and plans to continue to develop creative recipes for easy, healthy cooking.

Contents

This is a great collection of recipes for everyday meals at home as well as special dishes for friends and neighbors. All dishes are delicious and packed with lots of flavors so you don't miss out anything even though you are eating "healthy". And the best part...every recipe has only 4 ingredients!

Indicates Author's Choice Recipes

10 Things to Love About This Cookbook:

1. Diabetic recipes for every taste.
2. Food exchanges and nutritional analysis for every recipe.
3. Net-carb counts per serving.
4. Smart new products.
5. Easy, step-by-step instructions.
6. Quick and easy meal ideas.
7. Familiar and "comfort" foods prepared in healthier ways.
8. Incredible desserts.
9. Every recipe has only 4 ingredients
10. Incredible desserts.

Some Smart Products Used in This Cookbook:

Bagged lettuce and mixed salad greens

Boneless skinless chicken breasts

Campbell's® Healthy Request® condensed soups

Carb Options™ Asian Teriyaki Marinade

Carb Options™ Garden Style Sauce

Carb Options™ Olive Oil Vinaigrette Dressing

Carb Options™ Original Barbecue Sauce

Carb Options™ Super Chunk Peanut Spread

Egg Beaters® egg substitute

Frozen fruit

Frozen seasoning blends

Frozen vegetable blends

Light processed cheese

Light sour cream

Light mayonnaise

Lite frozen whipped topping

Lite soy sauce

Low-carb bread

Low-carb ice cream

Low-carb whole wheat tortillas

Low-carb yogurt

Mrs. Dash® seasoning blends

Murray® Sugar Free cookies

No-salt tomato sauce

Reduced-carb pasta

Reduced-fat cheddar/mozzarella cheese

Reduced-fat cream cheese

Reduced-fat graham cracker crusts

Russell Stover® Low Carb Peanut Butter Cups

Russell Stover® Low Carb Toffee Squares

Salt-free Creole seasoning

Smart Balance® Buttery Spread

Smuckers® Natural Creamy Peanut Butter

Smuckers® Sugar Free Hot Fudge Topping™

Splenda® sugar substitute

Sugar-free fruit spreads

Sugar-free gelatin mixes

Sugar-free pudding mixes

Sugar-free maple syrup

Swanson® Natural Goodness™ Chicken Broth

Whole wheat pasta (spaghetti, rotini)

Whole wheat tortillas

Whole wheat bread, crackers

Healthy Diets for Diabetics

People with diabetes have more food choices today than ever before.

In fact, the American Diabetes Association now maintains that the diabetic diet (low in refined carbohydrates, hydrogenated fat and sodium and rich in whole grains, fruits and vegetables including beans and peas) is essentially the healthy diet recommended for anyone interested in good nutrition.

Today's smart, convenient products make healthy eating easier by eliminating refined carbohydrates, reducing fat and sodium, and adding more whole grains. The recipes in this book use many of these smart products, plus plenty of fresh vegetables, meats and fruits for every taste. Each recipe includes serving size, nutritional analysis and food exchanges plus net carbs per serving.

Without guessing, reading labels or performing calculations, you can more easily follow your doctor's recommendations for calories, carbohydrates, protein, fat and other nutrients. Use this book as a guide in meal planning for the diabetic, low-carb dieter or anyone interested in no-fuss good nutrition.

This cookbook is not intended as a substitute for the advice of a physician. Always consult your doctor and/or registered dietitian for specific instructions regarding diabetic meal plans or weight loss programs.

Nutritional information was calculated using Nutritionist Pro™ analysis software by FirstDataBank. Nutritional calculations are approximate and do not include optional ingredients, garnishes or sauces, unless specifically stated in the recipe. When two or more ingredient choices are given, the ingredient listed first is the one used in nutritional analysis. Water, non-stick cooking spray, salt substitute and pepper are counted as "free" ingredients.

Brand name products used in this cookbook are the property of their respective owners, and no claim or endorsement is implied.

Nutritional references include publications by the American Diabetes Association and American Dietetic Association, along with Understanding Nutrition, 9th Ed. 2002, Whitney, E.N. & Rolfes, S.R. Belmont, CA: Wadsworth/Thomson Learning.

What are Net Carbs?

Simply put, net carbs, as defined in this cookbook, are the result of subtracting dietary fiber content from the total carbohydrate content in one serving of a food.

For example, if a label for one serving of bread lists 7 grams of total carbohydrates and 2 grams of dietary fiber, the result would be 5 grams of net carbs in one serving of bread.

In a few recipes, sugar alcohols are also subtracted from total carbohydrate content since they are listed on product labels. Keep in mind that sugar alcohols—NOT SUGARS—are subtracted from the total carbohydrate content.

The effect of sugar alcohols on total carbohydrate intake can be significant for the carb-conscious consumer. Researchers have reported that sugar alcohols, such as maltitol and sorbitol, are not chemically broken down in the body to glucose (sugar). If sugar alcohols appear on a product's label, manufacturers are subtracting sugar alcohols from the total carbohydrates in that product, further reducing the amount of net carbs.

For a person counting daily carbohydrate intake, understanding net carbs and how they are figured may be helpful.

■ ■ ■

What are Sugar Alcohols?

Sugar alcohols provide bulk and sweetness in chewing gums, candies, jams and jellies labeled as "sugar free." Sugar alcohols do provide some calories, but fewer calories than sugars. Sugar alcohols also occur naturally in fruits and vegetables. Examples of sugar alcohols are maltitol, mannitol, sorbitol, and xylitol. Compared to sugars, sugar alcohols are absorbed more slowly and are chemically broken down differently in the body. Look for sugar alcohols on the labels of sugarless gum and many sugar free and low carb sweets.

Because sugar alcohols are not completely absorbed, some (especially sorbitol and mannitol) may cause digestive discomfort for some people. The effects of sugar alcohols are related to the amount consumed, so read product labels and follow recommended serving size.

The Diabetes Food Pyramid

The Diabetes Food Pyramid is a handy way of remembering what foods you should eat every day. Based on the USDA Food Guide Pyramid, the Diabetes Food Pyramid has six main food groups and the recommended servings per day from each group. A healthy daily food plan for adults and adolescents includes servings from all the groups every day (except for Fats, Sweets & Alcohol Group).

Diabetes Pyramid Food Group .... **Servings Per Day**

Grains, Beans & Starchy Vegetables .... 6 or more

Vegetables .... 3 to 5

Fruits .... 2 to 4

Milk & Milk Products .... 2 to 3

Meat & Meat Substitutes .... 2 to 3

Fats, Sweets & Alcohol .... Small amounts

For more information, consult Exchange Lists for Meal Planning developed by the American Diabetes Association and the American Dietetic Association.

Food Exchanges

Food exchanges represent categories of foods grouped according to calories, fat, protein and carbohydrate content, and are derived from Exchange Lists for Meal Planning developed by the American Diabetes Association and the American Dietetic Association. A serving of a food in each group has about the same amount of carbohydrate, protein, fat and calories as other foods in the group.

Within a group, foods can be "exchanged" for one another. For example,
2 tablespoons of grated parmesan cheese and one ounce of lean pork are both equal to one lean meat exchange. Both foods have an average of 0 grams carbohydrate, 7 grams protein, 3 grams fat and 55 calories. In other words, 1 ounce of lean pork can be "exchanged" for 2 tablespoons parmesan cheese.

■ THE CARBOHYDRATE GROUP ■

The Carbohydrate Group includes the following food exchange lists:

Starch: (Cereal, grains, pasta, breads, peas, potatoes, cooked beans, peas, lentils)
One starch exchange equals 15 grams carbohydrate, 3 grams protein, 0 to 1 grams fat and 80 calories. Generally, one starch food exchange is:
  ½ cup cooked cereal
  ⅓ cup cooked rice or pasta
  1 ounce bread product, such as 1 slice bread

Fruit: (Fruit, unsweetened fruit juice)
One fruit exchange equals 15 grams carbohydrate and 60 calories. One fruit exchange is:
  1 small banana
  17 small grapes
  ½ cup orange juice

Milk: (Fat free, low fat, reduced fat, whole)
One milk exchange equals 12 grams carbohydrate and 8 grams protein. (Cheeses are on the Meat Food Exchange List and cream and other dairy fats are on the Fat Food Exchange List.) One milk food exchange is:
  1 cup fat free milk (0 to 3 grams fat per serving)
  1 cup 2% milk (5 grams fat per serving)
  1 cup whole milk (8 grams fat per serving) *continued on next page)*

Other Carbohydrates: (Sweets, desserts)
One other carbohydrate exchange equals 15 grams carbohydrate (or
1 starch or 1 fruit or 1 milk). One other carbohydrate exchange is:
   1 (2 inch square) brownie, unfrosted (1 other carbohydrate, 1 fat)
   ½ cup fat free no sugar added ice cream (1 other carbohydrate)

Nonstarchy Vegetables: (Broccoli, tomatoes, salad greens)
One vegetable exchange (½ cooked or 1 cup raw) equals 5 grams
carbohydrate,
2 grams protein, 0 grams fat and 5 calories. One vegetable exchange
is:
   ½ cup cooked mushrooms
   1 cup raw broccoli

▪ THE MEAT AND MEAT SUBSTITUTES GROUP ▪

Meat and meat substitutes containing both protein and fat are in this
group. Generally, 1 meat exchange is:
   1 ounce meat, poultry or cheese
   ½ cup beans, peas or lentils

Categories within this group are named based on servings of the
same amount of protein (7 grams), but differing amounts of fat and
calories.

The Meat and Meat Substitutes Group includes the following categories:

Very Lean Meat and Substitutes: (0 grams carbohydrate, 7 grams
protein, 0 to 1 grams fat, 35 calories) One ounce chicken or turkey
breast is 1 very lean meat exchange.

Lean Meat and Substitutes: (0 grams carbohydrate, 7 grams protein,
3 grams fat, 55 calories) One ounce ground round is 1 lean meat
exchange.

Medium Fat Meat and Substitutes: (0 grams carbohydrate, 7 grams
protein,
5 grams fat, 75 calories) One egg is 1 medium fat meat exchange.

High Fat Meat and Substitutes: (0 grams carbohydrate, 7 grams
protein, 8 grams fat, 100 calories) One ounce pork sausage is 1 high
fat meat exchange.

■ THE FAT GROUP ■

Based on the type of fat they contain, fats are divided into three groups: monounsaturated, polyunsaturated and saturated. In general, one fat exchange equals 5 grams fat and 45 calories:
1 teaspoon regular margarine
1 teaspoon vegetable oil
½ tablespoon peanut butter
1 teaspoon regular mayonnaise
1 tablespoon regular cream cheese

■ FREE FOOD EXCHANGES ■

A free food is any food or drink that contains less than 20 calories or 5 grams or fewer carbohydrates per serving. Check serving sizes of free foods and limit to
3 servings per day. Free foods include:
Fat-free or reduced-fat foods (1 tablespoon fat-free or reduced-fat sour cream)
Sugar free foods (2 teaspoons no sugar added jelly)
Drinks (Coffee and sugar-free diet soft drinks)
Condiments (lemon juice, mustard, ¼ cup salsa)
Seasonings (Fresh or dried herbs, garlic, flavoring extracts)

Diabetes Terms

Diabetes mellitus: A chronic disorder characterized by high blood glucose (sugar) resulting from insufficient or ineffective insulin production in the body.

Type 1 diabetes: A less common type of diabetes in which the body produces no insulin at all (also known as insulin-dependent diabetes mellitus or juvenile-onset diabetes).

Recommendations for Type 1 diabetes: To maintain appropriate blood glucose levels requires commitment to a carefully planned program of diet, physical activity and insulin injections, as directed by their physician or dietitian.

Type 2 diabetes: A more common type of diabetes characterized by high blood glucose and insulin resistance (also known as noninsulin-dependent diabetes mellitus or adult-onset diabetes).

Recommendations for Type 2 diabetes: Persons with Type 2 diabetes benefit most from a diet that controls blood glucose fluctuations and promotes weight loss. To maintain appropriate blood glucose levels, the same amount of carbohydrate should be consumed every day. Eating too much or too little carbohydrate can lead to problems. People with Type 2 diabetes should daily monitor the amount of their carbohydrate intake, as directed by their physician or dietitian.

Source: Whitney, E.N., & Rolfes, S. R. Understanding Nutrition, 9th ed. Belmont, CA: Wadsworth/Thomson Learning, 2002 (p. 620-624).

■ ■ ■

8 Ways to Reduce Salt Intake

1. Remove the salt shaker from the table!
2. Always taste foods before adding salt.
3. Cook with reduced-sodium or salt-free seasoning blends.
4. Use salt substitutes, such as those made with potassium chloride.
5. Use sodium-free herbs such as parsley, mint, basil, thyme, oregano and rosemary or herb blends.
6. Use sodium-free spices such as curry, ginger and pepper.
7. Use flavorings such as lemon juice, vinegar and wine.
8. Look for these product labels:
   Sodium-free, salt-free: less than 5 mg sodium per serving.
   Low-sodium: 140 mg or less per serving.
   Very low sodium: 35 mg or less per serving.

Sodium Q & A

Why do we like salt?
Salt gives food its own tangy taste, enhances other flavors and even suppresses bitter flavors. Throughout history, salt has been highly regarded. It simply tastes good!

How much sodium do I need?
Sodium is critical to bodily functions such as maintenance of balance of fluids, nerve transmissions and muscle contractions in the body.

Foods actually provide more sodium than the body needs. Our diets are rarely low in sodium. The minimum sodium requirement for adults is set at 500 milligrams in the United States. The maximum sodium requirement for adults is set at 2400 milligrams or 6 grams of sodium per day.

(continued on next page)

Which foods are low in sodium?
In general, unprocessed foods such as fresh fruits and vegetables have the least sodium. Milk and meats have moderate amounts of sodium.

Which foods should I avoid?
Processed foods generally have the most sodium. Researchers report that as much as 75% of the sodium in our diets comes from salt added to foods by manufacturers. About 15% comes from salt added during cooking and at the table. About 10% comes from the natural content in foods.

Use these products sparingly:
Salty snacks such as potato chips, pretzels, salted popcorn, salted nuts and crackers
Salty or smoked meats such as bacon, frankfurters, sausage, lunch meats and ham
Foods prepared in brine, such as pickles, olives and sauerkraut
Salty condiments such as seasoned salts, MSG, bouillon cubes, ketchup and mustard
Sauces such as soy, teriyaki, worcestershire and barbecue
Cheeses, especially processed cheeses
Canned and instant soups

■ ■ ■

Now you're cooking!

Good News About Splenda®

According to recent research, sucralose (found in Splenda®), like sugar alcohols, does not elevate blood sugar levels in the body. Findings were that sucralose and sugar alcohols do NOT contribute to the overall or "net" amount of carbohydrates in a serving of food.

~Dr. Sally Hunt

Cooking For Success

Read through the entire recipe:

Check nutritional analysis and food exchanges
Note preparation time required
Check ingredients list for specific preparation required (crushed, diced, sliced)
Check for use of water, salt substitute, pepper, and non-stick cooking spray ("free" ingredients)
Note optional ingredients or recipe variations
Note tools and cooking utensils (such as measuring spoons/cups, meat thermometer, non-stick skillet, wire mesh strainer, wire whisk)
Check procedures and order (such as preheating oven)

Assemble ingredients, tools and utensils needed:

Measure and/or prepare ingredients as directed
Check to see if you need a timer
Check to see if you need plastic wrap, aluminum foil, etc.
Check to see if you have the size of baking and/or serving dish required or can substitute

Prepare the recipe:

Follow recipe directions in order given
Follow times and temperatures for cooking
Follow methods for how food should be handled (mix, stir, toss)
Check descriptions of how to tell doneness of a food
Check to see if food should be served immediately or should be chilled before serving
Note suggested ways of serving (dessert plates or bowls, stemmed glasses)
Follow directions for serving sizes

Appetizers & Beverages

Rolled Enchilada Bites

Net Carbs: 4 g

1 (1 pound) package ground turkey breast or extra-lean
    ground beef
1 (10 ounce) can mild red chili enchilada sauce or Red Chili
    Enchilada Sauce, (p. 207)
8 (10 inch) low-carb whole wheat tortillas
2½ cups shredded reduced-fat cheddar or jack cheese

1. In sprayed heavy skillet over medium heat, cook and stir meat about 8 to 10 minutes. Remove meat from skillet. (If using beef, drain in wire mesh strainer and rinse to remove fat. Wipe skillet with paper towels.)

2. Preheat oven to 375°.

3. Return meat to skillet, add enchilada sauce and simmer 10 minutes over medium heat. Season to taste with salt substitute and pepper.

4. Spray both sides of each tortilla with cooking spray. Spread each tortilla with 2 tablespoons meat and 1 tablespoon cheese. Roll tightly.

5. On sprayed baking sheet, arrange rolled enchiladas seam side down. Spray enchiladas again with cooking spray.

6. Bake at 375° 10 to 15 minutes or until cheese melts. Cut each rolled enchilada into quarters and serve immediately.

Yield: 32 servings (32 enchilada quarters)   *Serving size: 1 quarter*
Calories: 115   *Protein: 10 g*   *Carbohydrate: 4 g*
Fat: 7 g   *Cholesterol: 25 mg*   *Sodium: 335 mg*
Calcium: 255 mg   *Fiber: less than 1 g*   *Sugars: 0 g*
Sugar Alcohol: 0 g
Food Exchanges: 1 medium fat meat, ½ bread

૨ Hot Asparagus Roll-Ups
Net Carbs: 11 g

10 fresh asparagus spears, trimmed
10 slices sugar-free wheat bread, crusts trimmed
1½ tablespoons light mayonnaise
5 reduced-fat mozzarella or cheddar string cheese sticks,
　pulled apart

1. In wide skillet, heat 1 inch water until it boils. Add asparagus, cover and cook 7 to 10 minutes. Do not overcook. Drain well and set aside.

2. With rolling pin, slightly flatten each trimmed bread slice. Spread about 1 teaspoon mayonnaise on one side of bread.

3. Top each bread slice with 1 or 2 asparagus spears and 3 to 4 cheese strings. Roll up carefully.

4. On sprayed baking sheet, arrange rolls seam side down and coat with cooking spray.

5. Broil 3 to 5 minutes about 5 inches below heat until bread toasts.

6. Serve immediately.

Yield: 10 servings　　　*Serving size: 1 roll*

Calories: 110　　　*Protein: 7 g*　　　*Carbohydrate: 14 g*
Fat: 3 g　　　*Cholesterol: 6 mg*　　　*Sodium: 218 mg*
Calcium: 86 mg　　　*Fiber: 3 g*　　　*Sugars: 1 g*
Sugar Alcohol: 0 g

Food Exchanges: 1½ bread, 1 vegetable, ½ fat

■ ■ ■

Zucchini Smiles

Net Carbs: 3 g

2 zucchini, sliced in ¾-inch thick slices
2 tablespoons bite-size crispy corn cereal squares, crushed
1 tablespoon grated parmesan or romano cheese
3 tablespoons light mayonnaise

1. In medium saucepan, heat ½ inch water until it boils. Add zucchini slices, reduce heat to simmer and cover.

2. Cook 3 to 5 minutes, just until zucchini becomes tender. Drain and cool on paper towels.

3. Mix crushed cereal and cheese. Spread mayonnaise evenly on one side of each zucchini slice. Coat that side with cheese mixture and spray lightly with cooking spray.

4. On sprayed baking sheet, broil zucchini slices 4 to 5 inches below heat source about 4 to 6 minutes.

5. Serve hot.

Yield: 7 servings (about 14 to 16 slices)   *Serving size: 2 slices*

Calories: 35   *Protein: less than 1 g*   *Carbohydrate: 3 g*
Fat: 2 g   *Cholesterol: 3 mg*   *Sodium: 60 mg*
Calcium: 18 mg   *Fiber: less than 1 g*   *Sugars: 1 g*
Sugar Alcohol: 0 g

Food Exchanges: ½ fat

■ ■ ■

Easy Porcupine Meatballs
Net Carbs: 16 g

1 (1 pound) package ground turkey or lean ground beef (or mixture
of turkey and beef)
1 (10 ounce) can Campbell's® Healthy Request® cream of
mushroom condensed soup
1 cup uncooked converted or parboiled long grain rice
⅓ cup chopped green onion

1. Preheat oven to 350°.

2. Combine all ingredients and mix well. Season to taste
with salt substitute and pepper.

3. Form meat mixture into balls of about 2 tablespoons
each. (For easier handling, spray hands with non-stick
cooking spray and scoop and pack mixture into ice
cream scoop.)

4. In sprayed 8-inch square baking dish, arrange
meatballs. Cover and bake 1 hour or until rice is tender.
(Parboiled or converted rice cooks in about 25 minutes.)

5. Uncover and bake 10 minutes or until meatballs brown.
Drain on paper towels, then serve or freeze for later use.

*Optional: Serve with no-salt tomato sauce, Carb Options™
garden-style pasta sauce or Carb Options™ alfredo
sauce.*

Yield: 10 to 12 servings   Serving size: 1 meatball

Calories: 140   Protein: 9 g   Carbohydrate: 16 g
Fat: 4 g   Cholesterol: 34 mg   Sodium: 126 mg
Calcium: 40 mg   Fiber: less than 1 g   Sugars: less than 1 g
Sugar Alcohol: 0 g

Food Exchanges: 1 bread, 1 other carb, ½ medium fat meat

Saucy Chicken Wings

Net Carbs: less than 1 g

20 frozen chicken wing sections, thawed
Salt-free Creole seasoning to taste
Garlic powder to taste
½ to 1 cup Carb Options™ barbecue sauce

1. Preheat oven to 325°.

2. On sprayed foil-lined baking sheet, arrange chicken wings. Sprinkle with seasonings and pepper to taste.

3. Brush wings with barbecue sauce and bake at 325° for about 30 minutes.

4. Turn wings over and brush other sides with sauce. Return to oven and bake 30 more minutes or until chicken is fork-tender and crisp.

Yield: 10 servings   *Serving size: 2 pieces*

Calories: 62   *Protein: 5 g*   *Carbohydrate: less than 1 g*
Fat: 5 g   *Cholesterol: 24 mg*   *Sodium: 153 mg*
Calcium: 0 mg   *Fiber: 0 g*   *Sugars: 0 g*
Sugar Alcohol: 0 g

Food Exchanges: ½ medium fat meat

■ ■ ■

Veggie Nachos
Net Carbs: 3 g

4 cups cut vegetables
1½ cups finely shredded reduced-fat cheddar or jack cheese
2 to 3 tablespoons canned mild diced green chilies, drained
2 to 3 tablespoons sliced ripe olives, drained

1. Preheat broiler. On ovenproof serving platter, arrange vegetable pieces (celery and carrot sticks, squash slices, bell pepper strips, cauliflower and broccoli florets) and sprinkle with cheese, chilies and olives.

2. Broil 4 to 6 inches from heat about 5 to 7 minutes or until cheese melts. Serve immediately.

Yield: 6 to 8 servings   *Serving size: ½ cup*

Calories: 180   *Protein: 13 g*   *Carbohydrate: 5 g*
Fat: 13 g   *Cholesterol: 35 mg*   *Sodium: 419 mg*
Calcium: 380 mg   *Fiber: 2 g*   *Sugars: 3 g*
Sugar Alcohol: 0 g

Food Exchanges: 1½ fat, ½ medium fat meat, ½ vegetable

■ ■ ■

⅜ Neptune's Favorite Shrimp Dip

Net Carbs: 1 g

This delicious dip disappears quickly!

1 (8 ounce) package reduced-fat cream cheese (Neufchatel)
½ cup light mayonnaise
1 (6 ounce) can peeled-veined shrimp, drained, rinsed, chopped or
**   1 cup frozen peeled-veined shrimp, slightly thawed**
1½ teaspoons salt-free Creole seasoning

1. To soften cheese for mixing, remove foil wrapper and place in small microwave-safe bowl. Heat on HIGH power about 5 seconds.

2. Stir in mayonnaise. Add shrimp and seasoning blend and mix well. Chill 1 hour before serving.

Yield: 18 servings (About 2¼ cups)   *Serving size: 2*
     tablespoons

Calories: 66   *Protein: 3 g*   *Carbohydrate: 1 g*
Fat: 5 g   *Cholesterol: 28 mg*   *Sodium: 106 mg*
Calcium: 15 mg   *Fiber: 0 g*   *Sugars: less than 1 g*
Sugar Alcohol: 0 g

Food Exchanges: ½ fat

■ ■ ■

Party Cheese Squares
Net Carbs: 1 g

4 cups shredded reduced-fat cheddar cheese
1 cup Egg Beaters® egg substitute
1 (4 ounce) can mild diced green chilies, drained
⅓ cup finely chopped green onions with tops

1. Preheat oven to 325°. Mix all ingredients and spread into sprayed 8 x 8-inch square baking dish.

2. Bake 30 minutes or until table knife inserted in middle comes out clean. Cut into 1½-inch squares and serve hot.

Yield: 25 servings (about 25 squares)   *Serving size: 1 square*
Calories: 128   *Protein: 10 g*   *Carbohydrate: 2 g*
Fat: 9 g   *Cholesterol: 26 mg*   *Sodium: 419 mg*
Calcium: 315 mg   *Fiber: 1 g*   *Sugars: less than 1 g*
Sugar Alcohol: 0 g   *Food Exchanges: 0*

■ ■ ■

Low-Fat Hummus
Net Carbs: 7 g

1 (16 ounce) can garbanzos (chickpeas)
½ cup non-fat plain yogurt
3 teaspoons fresh lemon juice
⅛ to ¼ teaspoon garlic powder

1. Drain and rinse garbanzos in cold water.

2. With food processor, process all ingredients until smooth.

Yield: About 12 servings   *Serving size: 2 tablespoons*
Calories: 52   *Protein: 2 g*   *Carbohydrate: 9 g*
Fat: less than 1 g   *Cholesterol: less than 1 mg*   *Sodium: 121 mg*
Calcium: 29 mg   *Fiber: 2 g*   *Sugars: 3 g*
Sugar Alcohol: 0 g   *Food Exchanges: ½ bread*

Chickpea Party Appetizer
Net Carbs: 11 g

Low-Fat Hummus (p. 25)
¼ cup chopped roasted red pepper or diced pimiento, drained
¼ cup chopped red onion
¼ cup crumbled feta cheese

1. In shallow dish or plate, spread hummus evenly and sprinkle with pepper, red onions and feta cheese.

Tip: Serve with pita bread wedges or crisp bread sticks.

Yield: 8 to 10 servings   *Serving size: About ¼ cup*

Calories: 81   *Protein: 4 g*   *Carbohydrate: 13 g*
Fat: 2 g   *Cholesterol: 3 mg*   *Sodium: 204 mg*
Calcium: 48 mg   *Fiber: 2 g*   *Sugars: 4 g*
Sugar Alcohol: 0 g

Food Exchanges: ½ bread, ½ medium fat meat

■ ■ ■

❧ Hot Artichoke Appetizer

Net Carbs: 3 g

2 (8.5 ounce) cans artichoke hearts in water, drained, chopped
1 (4 ounce) can mild diced green chilies, drained
6 tablespoons light mayonnaise
1½ cups finely shredded reduced-fat cheddar cheese

1. Preheat oven to 350°. In sprayed 11 x 7-inch baking dish, spread chopped artichokes and top with chilies. Carefully spread mayonnaise over chilies and sprinkle with cheese.

2. Cover and bake 15 minutes or until mixture bubbles and heats through. Serve immediately.

Yield: 20 servings (About 2½ cups)   *Serving size: 2*
                                             tablespoons

Calories: 79   *Protein: 5 g*   *Carbohydrate: 3 g*
Fat: 6 g   *Cholesterol: 14 mg*   *Sodium: 232 mg*
Calcium: 126 mg   *Fiber: less than 1 g*   *Sugars: less than 1 g*
Sugar Alcohol: 0 g

Food Exchanges: ½ fat

■ ■ ■

Dippy Spinach Special
Net Carbs: 2 g

1 (10 ounce) package frozen chopped spinach, thawed
⅓ cup green onions with tops, finely chopped
1 tablespoon fresh lemon juice
1 (8 ounce) carton light sour cream

1. In wire mesh strainer, drain spinach and squeeze out as much liquid as possible. In food processor or blender, process all ingredients until smooth. Season to taste with salt substitute and pepper.

2. Cover and chill at least 2 hours before serving.

Yield: 16 servings (About 2 cups)   *Serving size: 2 tablespoons*

Calories: 23   *Protein: 1 g*   *Carbohydrate: 2 g*
Fat: 1 g   *Cholesterol: 5 mg*   *Sodium: 34 mg*
Calcium: 42 mg   *Fiber: less than 1 g* *Sugars: 1 g*
Sugar Alcohol: 0 g

Food Exchanges: 0

■ ■ ■

Pita Crisps
Net Carbs: 8 g

4 whole wheat pita breads

1. Preheat oven to 350°. With sharp knife, cut each pita bread to make 12 single wedges. Spray wedges lightly with cooking spray. Place wedges on baking sheet.

2. Bake 8 to10 minutes or until wedges are light brown and crisp. Serve immediately or store in airtight container.

Optional: Before baking, sprinkle wedges with herb or spice of your choice.

Yield: 16 servings (48 wedges)   *Serving size: 3 wedges*

Calories: 43	*Protein: 2 g*	*Carbohydrate: 9 g*
Fat: less than 1 g	*Cholesterol: 0 mg*	*Sodium: 85 mg*
Calcium: 2 mg	*Fiber: 1 g*	*Sugars: less than 1 g*
Sugar Alcohol: 0 g		

Food Exchanges: ½ bread

■ ■ ■

❧ No-Guilt Tortilla Crisps

Net Carbs: 4 g

12 (8 inch) low-carb whole wheat tortillas
Non-stick cooking spray

1. Preheat oven to 325°. In batches, stack and cut tortillas into 6 wedges. Place on wax paper or parchment paper and spray with non-stick cooking spray on both sides.

2. On sprayed baking sheet, bake wedges at 325° for 20 to 30 minutes or until they brown and become crisp. Cool and store in airtight container.

Yield: 12 servings (72 wedges)   *Serving size: 4 to 6 wedges*

Calories: 70   *Protein: 4 g*   *Carbohydrate: 7 g*
Fat: 4 g   *Cholesterol: 0 mg*   *Sodium: 250 mg*
Calcium: 0 mg   *Fiber: 3 g*   *Sugars: 0 g*
Sugar Alcohol: 0 g

Food Exchanges: 1 fat, ½ bread

■ ■ ■

Wakka-Moley

Net Carbs: 2 g

2 ripe avocados
1 teaspoon grated onion
2 teaspoons fresh lime juice
¼ teaspoon garlic salt or powder

1. Halve avocados and remove seeds. Cut halves into quarters and peel. Mash avocado with fork.

2. Combine all ingredients. If using garlic powder, season to taste with salt substitute. Cover tightly until ready to serve.

Optional: Serve with No-Guilt Tortilla Crisps (p. 30)

Yield: 4 servings (about 1 cup)   *Serving size: ¼ cup*

Calories: 143   *Protein: 2 g*   *Carbohydrate: 8 g*
Fat: 13 g   *Cholesterol: 0 mg*   *Sodium: 67 mg*
Calcium: 11 mg   *Fiber: 6 g*   *Sugars: less than 1 g*
Sugar Alcohol: 0 g

Food Exchanges: 2½ fat, 1 vegetable

■ ■ ■

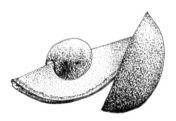

⅋ Sesame-Cheddar Balls

Net Carbs: 1 g

1 (8 ounce) package reduced-fat cream cheese (Neufchatel)
2 (8 ounce) packages finely shredded reduced-fat cheddar cheese
2 tablespoons finely chopped green onions with tops
3 tablespoons sesame seeds

1. In mixing bowl, mix cream cheese, cheddar cheese and green onions. Cover and chill at least 4 hours.

2. In dry skillet over medium heat, stir and toast sesame seeds until seeds are golden brown and fragrant. Remove from heat and cool. Form cheese mixture into 1-inch balls and roll in toasted sesame seeds. Chill before serving.

Yield: 12 servings (about 2½ cups)   *Serving size: 2 balls*

Calories: 178   *Protein: 12 g*   *Carbohydrate: 1 g*
Fat: 14 g   *Cholesterol: 40 mg*   *Sodium: 350 mg*
Calcium: 301 mg   *Fiber: less than 1 g*   *Sugars: less than 1 g*
Sugar Alcohol: 0 g

Food Exchanges: 1 fat, ½ medium fat meat

■ ■ ■

Perfect Deviled Eggs

Net Carbs: less than 1 g

Everybody's favorite!

6 eggs
3 tablespoons light or fat-free mayonnaise
2 teaspoons dijon-style or yellow mustard
⅛ to ¼ teaspoon salt-free Creole or other seasoning, divided

1. To prevent cracking, set eggs at room temperature 10 to 15 minutes before cooking.

2. In large saucepan, heat 4 inches water until it boils. With large spoon, carefully lower each egg into boiling water.

3. Maintain medium boil and continue to cook eggs for 10 minutes. Remove eggs and plunge into cold or ice water.

4. Carefully crack shells all around eggs. Remove shells from eggs and slice eggs in half lengthwise.

5. With fork, carefully remove and thoroughly mash egg yolks. Add mayonnaise, mustard and seasoning to yolks. Beat together with fork until mixture is creamy and smooth.

6. Mound egg yolk mixture evenly into cooked egg whites, covering egg yolk holes. Sprinkle each yolk with dash seasoning. Cover and chill before serving.

Yield: 12 servings   *Serving size: 1 deviled egg half*

Calories: 52   *Protein: 3 g*   *Carbohydrate: less than 1 g*
Fat: 4 g   *Cholesterol: 107 mg*   *Sodium: 74 mg*
Calcium: 14 mg   *Fiber: 0 g*   *Sugars: less than 1 g*
Sugar Alcohol: 0 g   *Food Exchanges: ½ medium fat meat*

Snappy Chicken Spread
Net Carbs: 2 g

1 cup chopped cooked chicken breast
¼ to ⅓ cup light mayonnaise
½ cup sliced celery
¼ cup diced pimento with liquid

1. In food processor or blender, combine all ingredients until they mix well.

2. Season to taste with salt substitute and pepper.

Yield: 6 servings (about 1½ cups)   *Serving size: ¼ cup*

Calories: 58	*Protein: 7 g*	*Carbohydrate: 2 g*
Fat: 2 g	*Cholesterol: 20 mg*	*Sodium: 110 mg*
Calcium: 7 mg	*Fiber: less than 1 g*	*Sugars: less than 1 g*
Sugar Alcohol: 0 g	*Food Exchanges: ½ lean meat*	

Jezebel's Cream Cheese Spread
Net Carbs: 4 g

½ cup low-sugar apricot fruit spread
1 to 2 tablespoons prepared horseradish
1 (8 ounce) package reduced fat cream cheese (Neufchatel)

1. Mix fruit spread, horseradish and ¼ teaspoon ground black pepper.

2. Spoon over block of cream cheese.

Yield: 16 servings (about 2 cups) Serving size: 2 tablespoons cheese with sauce

Calories: 49	*Protein: 2 g*	*Carbohydrate: 4 g*
Fat: 3 g	*Cholesterol: 10 mg*	*Sodium: 63 mg*
Calcium: 11 mg	*Fiber: less than 1 g*	*Sugars: 3 g*
Sugar Alcohol: 0 g	*Food Exchanges: ½ fat*	

California-Dreamin' Tuna Spread

Net Carbs: 1 g

2 large avocados, pitted, peeled, slightly mashed
1 (6 ounce) can solid white albacore tuna in water, drained
2 tablespoons fresh lemon juice
2 teaspoons prepared horseradish

1. Combine all ingredients and mix well. Cover tightly
   and chill before serving.

Optional: *Add dash bottled hot pepper sauce or salt-free
Creole seasoning.*

Yield: 8 servings (2 cups)   Serving size: ¼ cup

Calories: 100   Protein: 7 g   Carbohydrate: 4 g
Fat: 7 g   Cholesterol: 10 g   Sodium: 101 mg
Calcium: 8 mg   Fiber: 3 g   Sugars: less than 1 g
Sugar Alcohol: 0 g

Food Exchanges: 1 medium fat meat, ½ fat

■ ■ ■

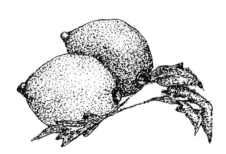

Chickpea Hummus

Net Carbs: 14 g

2 cloves garlic, minced
1 (15 ounce) can chickpeas (garbanzo beans), drained, rinsed
1 tablespoon sesame seeds, toasted
2 to 2½ tablespoons fresh lemon juice

1. In sprayed skillet over medium heat, cook and stir garlic 1 to 2 minutes. In food processor, blend all ingredients until smooth. Season to taste with salt substitute and pepper. Chill 1 to 2 hours for flavors to blend.

Tip: Use 2 to 3 tablespoons tahini (sesame seed paste) instead of sesame seeds if you prefer.

Optional: Serve with Pita Crisps (p. 29)

Yield: 6 servings (about 1½ cups)   *Serving size: ¼ cup*

Calories: 96   *Protein: 4 g*   *Carbohydrate: 17 g*
Fat: 2 g   *Cholesterol: 0 mg*   *Sodium: 212 mg*
Calcium: 40 mg   *Fiber: 3 g*   *Sugars: 4 g*
Sugar Alcohol: 0 g

Food Exchanges: 1 bread, ½ fat

■ ■ ■

Frosty Strawberry Soda

Net Carbs: 14 g

1½ cups skim milk
1½ cups sliced fresh strawberries
2 cups no-sugar-added strawberry ice cream
1 (16 ounce) bottle club soda

1. In blender, process milk and strawberries 10 to 15 seconds. Pour into 5 tall glasses.

2. Add small scoop strawberry ice cream to each glass. Slowly add soda to fill about ½ inch from top of glass.

3. Serve immediately with straw and iced teaspoon.

Tip: If you like, use 1 (10 ounce) package unsweetened sliced strawberries, partially thawed, instead of fresh strawberries.

Optional: Garnish with fresh strawberry.

Variation: To reduce net carbs, substitute low-carb ice cream.

Yield: 6 servings   *Serving size: About 1 cup*

Calories: 92   *Protein: 4 g*   *Carbohydrate: 14 g*
Fat: 2 g   *Cholesterol: 8 mg*   *Sodium: 77 mg*
Calcium: 101 mg   *Fiber: less than 1 g*   *Sugars: 7 g*
Sugar Alcohol: 0 g

Food Exchanges: ½ milk, ½ fruit

Whole fruit is more filling than fruit juice and generally has more fiber.

Raspberry-Pineapple Freeze
Net Carbs: 19 g

The ice cubes turn into pink punch as they melt!

1 (.3 ounce) packet sugar-free raspberry soft drink mix
½ cup Splenda® sugar substitute
4 cups unsweetened pineapple juice
2 to 3 (12 ounce) cans diet lemon-lime soda, chilled

1. In large bowl, mix soft drink powder, sugar substitute and juice. Pour into 2 ice cube trays and freeze.

2. To serve, place cubes in glasses and fill with diet soda.

Yield: 8 servings (24 cubes)   Serving size: 3 cubes

Calories: 75
Fat: less than 1 g
Calcium: 21 mg
Sugar Alcohol: 0 g

Protein: less than 1 g
Cholesterol: 0 mg
Fiber: less than 1 g

Carbohydrate: 19 g
Sodium: 12 mg
Sugars: 17 g

Food Exchanges: 1 fruit

■ ■ ■

Skinny Black Cow
Net Carbs: 19 g

1 (12 ounce) can diet root beer, chilled
½ cup no-sugar-added vanilla ice cream

1. Into tall 10-ounce glass, pour diet root beer. Top with ice cream.

2. Serve immediately with straw and iced teaspoon.

Variation: To reduce net carbs, substitute low-carb ice cream.

Yield: 1 serving	*Serving size: 1½ cups*	
Calories: 91	*Protein: 3 g*	*Carbohydrate: 19 g*
Fat: 0 g	*Cholesterol: 0 mg*	*Sodium: 122 mg*
Calcium: 80 mg	*Fiber: 0 g*	*Sugars: 4 g*
Sugar Alcohol: 0 g	*Food Exchanges: 0*	

Old-Time Lemonade
Net Carbs: 8 g

1 cup Splenda® sugar substitute
1 cup fresh lemon juice
Lemon slices for garnish
Mint sprigs for garnish

1. In large pitcher, combine sugar substitute, lemon juice and 1 cup water and stir until sugar substitute dissolves. Add 4 cups water. Serve over ice with lemon slices and mint sprigs.

Yield: 6 servings (about 6½ cups)		*Serving size: 1 cup*
Calories: 10	*Protein: less than 1 g*	*Carbohydrate: 8 g*
Fat: 0 g	*Cholesterol: 0 mg*	*Sodium: less than 1 mg*
Calcium: 3 mg	*Fiber: less than 1 g*	*Sugars: less than 1 g*
Sugar Alcohol: 0 g	*Food Exchanges: 0*	

Lemon-Lime Punch Smoothie

Net Carbs: 8 g

1 (.3 ounce) packet sugar-free lemon-lime soft drink mix
4 cups skim milk
2 cups no-sugar-added vanilla ice cream or frozen yogurt
1 to 2 (12 ounce) cans diet lemon-lime soda

1. In large punch bowl, combine soft drink mix with milk and stir until it dissolves. Add ice cream or yogurt in small spoonfuls.

2. Carefully pour soda down side of punch bowl. Stir gently with vertical motion. Serve immediately.

Yield: 15 servings (about 7½ cups)   *Serving size: ½ cup*

Calories: 48   *Protein: 3 g*   *Carbohydrate: 8 g*
Fat: less than 1 g   *Cholesterol: 1 mg*   *Sodium: 44 mg*
Calcium: 81 mg   *Fiber: 0 g*   *Sugars: 4 g*
Sugar Alcohol: 0 g

Food Exchanges: ½ milk

■ ■ ■

Fruit Tea Fizz

Net Carbs: 5 g

Make this really fast with the new cold brew tea bags!

5 to 6 (regular size) or 2 to 3 (family size) decaffeinated tea bags
½ cup Splenda® sugar substitute
1 cup fresh orange juice
1½ (12 ounce) cans diet lemon-lime soda or 2 to 3 cups club soda

1. In large saucepan, pour 3 cups boiling water over tea bags. Cover and let stand 5 minutes. Remove tea bags. Add sugar substitute and stir until it dissolves.

2. Add orange juice and pour into pitcher with 2 cups ice cubes.

3. Just before serving, carefully pour soda down side of pitcher.

Variation: Substitute ½ cup orange juice and ⅓ cup fresh lemon juice for 1 cup orange juice. Substitute 1 cup reduced-calorie cranberry juice cocktail for 1 cup orange juice.

Yield: 8 servings (8 cups)   *Serving size: 1 cup*

Calories: 15   *Protein: less than 1 g*   *Carbohydrate: 5 g*
Fat: less than 1 g   *Cholesterol: 0 mg*   *Sodium: 10 mg*
Calcium: 3 mg   *Fiber: less than 1 g*   *Sugars: 0 g*
Sugar Alcohol: 0 g

Food Exchanges: 0

■ ■ ■

Sugar-Free Hot Cocoa

Net Carbs: 11 g

4 tablespoons unsweetened cocoa
2 tablespoons Splenda® sugar substitute
3¼ cups skim milk
½ teaspoon vanilla

1. In medium heavy saucepan, mix cocoa and sugar substitute. Over medium heat, add ½ cup milk, stirring constantly with wire whisk until dry ingredients dissolve.

2. Gradually add remaining milk and cook and stir just until cocoa bubbles. Remove from heat and stir in vanilla. Serve immediately.

Optional: Top with ground cinnamon or nutmeg.

Yield: 4 servings   *Serving size: ¾ cup*

Calories: 79   *Protein: 8 g*   *Carbohydrate: 13 g*
Fat: less than 1 g   *Cholesterol: 4 mg*   *Sodium: 89 mg*
Calcium: 188 mg   *Fiber: 2 g*   *Sugars: 10 g*
Sugar Alcohol: 0 g

Food Exchanges: ½ milk, ½ other carb

■ ■ ■

Hot Cranberry Tea
Net Carbs: 11 g

Clove-Cinnamon Spice Mix (p. 44)
⅓ cup Splenda® sugar substitute
1 cup reduced-calorie cranberry juice cocktail
4 (regular size) decaffeinated tea bags

1. In saucepan, heat 1 cup water until it boils and add Clove-Cinnamon Spice Mix. Reduce heat, cover and simmer 10 minutes. Add 1 cup water, sugar substitute and cranberry juice and heat to boiling again.

2. Remove from heat, add tea bags and cover. Let stand 5 minutes. Remove tea bags and spice mix and serve.

Yield: 3 servings (about 3 cups)   *Serving size: 1 cup*

Calories: 56   *Protein: less than 1 g*   *Carbohydrate: 14 g*
Fat: 2 g   *Cholesterol: 0 mg*   *Sodium: 49 mg*
Calcium: 80 mg   *Fiber: 3 g*   *Sugars: 4 g*
Sugar Alcohol: 0 g

Food Exchanges: 1 fruit

■ ■ ■

Hot Spicy Orange Tea

Net Carbs: 13 g

Clove-Cinnamon Spice Mix (below)
⅓ cup Splenda® sugar substitute
1 cup fresh orange juice
4 (regular size) decaffeinated tea bags

1. In saucepan, heat 1 cup water until it boils and add Clove-Cinnamon Spice Mix.

2. Reduce heat, cover and simmer 10 minutes. Add 1 cup water, sugar substitute and orange juice and heat to boiling again.

3. Remove from heat, add tea bags and cover. Let stand 5 minutes. Remove tea bags and spice mix and serve.

Yield: 3 servings   *Serving size: 1 cup*

Calories: 48   *Protein: less than 1 g*   *Carbohydrate: 13 g*
Fat: less than 1 g   *Cholesterol: 0 mg*   *Sodium: 12 mg*
Calcium: 27 mg   *Fiber: less than 1 g*   *Sugars: less than 1 g*
Sugar Alcohol: 0 g

Food Exchanges: 1 fruit

Clove-Cinnamon Spice Mix

10 whole cloves
1 cinnamon stick, broken
Metal tea holder, ball or cheesecloth square

1. Place cloves and cinnamon in metal tea holder or ball or tie in cheesecloth square.

Yield: Mix for 2 cups tea

Breakfast & Brunch

Breakfast-Yogurt Parfait

Net Carbs: 21 g

½ cup fresh blueberries
½ cup sliced fresh strawberries
1 (6 ounce) carton low-carb strawberry yogurt, divided
¼ cup high-fiber, high-protein granola cereal

1. Combine blueberries and strawberries and place ¼ cup fruit mixture in each of 2 tall parfait glass. Top fruit with 3 tablespoons yogurt and half the cereal.

2. Add remaining fruit, reserve a few pieces for garnish. Top with remaining yogurt and garnish with reserved fruit.

Tip: If you do not have fresh fruit, try ½ cup frozen blueberries, slightly thawed, and ½ cup frozen sliced strawberries, slightly thawed.

Yield: 2 servings   *Serving size: 1 parfait*

Calories: 191   *Protein: 10 g*   *Carbohydrate: 28 g*
Fat: 3 g   *Cholesterol: 8 mg*   *Sodium: 145 mg*
Calcium: 33 mg   *Fiber: 7 g*   *Sugars: 14 g*
Sugar Alcohol: 0 g

Food Exchanges: 1 bread, ½ fruit, ½ milk, ½ fat

■ ■ ■

Cantaloupe Fruit Bowl

Net Carbs: 34 g

2 small cantaloupes
1 cup honeydew melon balls
1 cup canned pineapple tidbits in juice, drained, chilled
1 cup fresh blueberries

1. Halve cantaloupes stem end to stem end and remove seeds with spoon. With melon baller, scoop balls from inside cantaloupe.

2. Arrange cantaloupe balls, honeydew balls, and drained pineapple tidbits in cantaloupe halves. Sprinkle tops with blueberries. Cover and chill. Serve within 1 to 2 hours for best results.

Yield: 4 servings   *Serving size: ½ cantaloupe with fruit*

Calories: 151   *Protein: 3 g*   *Carbohydrate: 38 g*
Fat: less than 1 g   *Cholesterol: 0 mg*   *Sodium: 54 mg*
Calcium: 27 mg   *Dietary Fiber: 4 g*   *Sugars: 33 g*
Sugar Alcohol: 0 g

Food Exchanges: 2½ fruit

■ ■ ■

Good Morning Grapefruit
Net Carbs: 11 g

2 large grapefruit, halved
2 tablespoons Smart Balance® buttery spread
Few drops orange extract or ½ teaspoon cinnamon
2 teaspoons Splenda® sugar substitute

1. With grapefruit knife or paring knife, section each grapefruit half by cutting around each section close to membrane. Sections should be loosened from shell completely.

2. In small saucepan, melt buttery spread or melt in microwave. Add orange extract and sugar substitute and mix well. Drizzle over grapefruit halves.

3. In shallow baking pan about 4 inches from heat, broil grapefruit halves until tops bubble and turn light brown.

Tip: If you can find pink grapefruit, they are usually sweeter.

Yield: 4 servings   Serving size: 1 grapefruit half

Calories: 92   Protein: less than 1 g   Carbohydrate: 13 g
Fat: 5 g   Cholesterol: 0 mg   Sodium: 45 mg
Calcium: 27 mg   Fiber: 2 g   Sugars: 8 g
Sugar Alcohol: 0 g

Food Exchanges: 1 fat, ½ fruit, ½ other carb

■ ■ ■

Zucchini Frittata

Net Carbs: 3 g

A frittata is a baked flat omelet with vegetables and herbs.

1 cup frozen pepper stir-fry vegetables (red, green, yellow bell
    peppers and onions)
1 zucchini, shredded
1 cup Egg Beaters® egg substitute
¼ teaspoon crushed dried basil

1. Preheat oven to 350°. In preheated sprayed skillet, cook and stir peppers until water evaporates. Stir in shredded zucchini and cook 1 more minute. Drain in wire strainer.

2. In mixing bowl, combine all ingredients and season to taste with black pepper and salt or salt substitute.

3. In sprayed non-stick 9-inch pie pan, pour mixture and bake 25 minutes or until frittata sets and edges begin to brown.

4. With knife, loosen frittata around edges. Turn out onto plate and cut into four wedges. Serve hot or at room temperature.

Tip: Serve with salsa.

Yield: 4 servings   *Serving size: ¼ frittata*

Calories: 45   *Protein: 7 g*   *Carbohydrate: 4 g*
Fat: 0 g   *Cholesterol: 0 mg*   *Sodium: 125 mg*
Calcium: 32 mg   *Fiber: 1 g*   *Sugars: 2 g*
Sugar Alcohol: 0 g

Food Exchanges: 1 vegetable, 1 very lean meat

■ ■ ■

Fancy Seafood Grits
Net Carbs: 26 g

1 cup quick-cooking grits
¼ cup chopped green onions with tops
1 pound fresh or 1 (16 ounce) package frozen shrimp, peeled, veined
Grated parmesan cheese with basil, garlic and parsley

1. Cook grits according to package instructions for 4 servings. Set aside and keep warm.

2. In sprayed non-stick skillet over medium heat, cook and stir green onions about 1 minute. Add shrimp and cook and stir about 5 minutes or until shrimp turn pink. Season to taste with salt substitute and pepper.

3. To serve, spoon ½ cup cooked grits on each plate. Spoon shrimp-green onion mixture evenly over grits and sprinkle with cheese.

Yield: 5 to 6 servings   *Serving size: ½ cup*

Calcium: 213 g   *Protein: 21 g*   *Carbohydrate: 26 g*
Fat: 2 g   *Cholesterol: 138 mg*   *Sodium: 145 mg*
Calcium: 58 mg   *Fiber: less than 1 g*   *Sugars: less than 1 g*
Sugar Alcohol: 0 g

Food Exchanges: 2 bread, 2 lean meat

■ ■ ■

Breakfast-Bacon Scramble

Net Carbs: 2 g

¼ cup Egg Beaters® egg substitute
2 tablespoons low-fat small curd cottage cheese, drained
1 teaspoon Smart Balance® buttery spread
1 slice turkey bacon, cooked, crumbled

1. Mix egg substitute and cottage cheese. Season to taste with salt substitute and pepper.

2. In sprayed skillet over medium heat, melt buttery spread and heat until it bubbles.

3. Stir in egg mixture and cook and stir until eggs are soft-scrambled. Remove from skillet and drain if needed.

4. Sprinkle with crumbled turkey bacon and serve immediately.

Optional: Add 2 to 3 dashes hot pepper sauce.

Yield: 1 serving   *Serving size: ⅓ cup*

Calories: 112   *Protein: 12 g*   *Carbohydrate: 2 g*
Fat: 6 g   *Cholesterol: 12 mg*   *Sodium: 450 mg*
Calcium: 40 mg   *Fiber: 0 g*   *Sugars: less than 1 g*
Sugar Alcohol: 0 g

Food Exchanges: ½ medium fat meat, ½ fat

◆

Egg substitutes are made mostly from egg whites, contain less fat than whole eggs, and have no cholesterol. Use ¼ cup refrigerated egg substitute for 1 whole egg.

Southern Brunch Ham and Rice

Net Carbs: 18 g

This recipe is an excellent way to use leftover rice.

2 cups frozen seasoning blend (celery, onion, peppers, parsley)
8 slices 98% fat-free deli ham, diced
2 cups cooked long grain white or brown rice
½ cup Egg Beaters® egg substitute

1. To non-stick skillet over medium heat, add 1 to 2 tablespoons water and frozen seasoning blend. Cook and stir until vegetables are tender, adding more water if needed. Continue cooking and stirring until liquid evaporates.

2. Spray vegetables and skillet with nonstick cooking spray. Add ham and cook 1 to 2 minutes.

3. Stir in rice and mix well. Pour in egg substitute and continue to cook and stir until it sets. Season to taste with salt substitute and pepper.

4. Serve warm.

Yield: 6 servings (about 3 cups)   *Serving size: ½ cup*

Calories: 110   *Protein: 6 g*   *Carbohydrate: 18 g*
Fat: less than 1 g   *Cholesterol: 8 mg*   *Sodium: 200 mg*
Calcium: 12 mg   *Fiber: less than 1 g*   *Sugars: 2 g*
Sugar Alcohol: 0 g

Food Exchanges: 2 bread, 1 vegetable

■ ■ ■

Cheesy Southern Grits

Net Carbs: 14 g

1¾ cups Swanson Natural Goodness® chicken broth
½ cup quick-cooking grits
¼ cup Egg Beaters® egg substitute
1 cup finely shredded reduced-fat cheddar cheese

1 Preheat oven to 325°.

2. In medium saucepan, heat broth until it boils. Slowly stir grits into boiling broth. Reduce heat to simmer, then cover and cook 5 minutes. Remove from heat.

3. While stirring, slowly add Egg Beaters® to grits and mix well. Add shredded cheese and stir until cheese melts.

4. Spray 1-quart baking dish with non-stick spray, then add grits. Bake for 30 to 35 minutes and let stand 5 minutes before serving.

Optional: Sprinkle grits with paprika for color.

Yield: 4 servings   *Serving size: ½ cup*

Calories: 261   *Protein: 18 g*   *Carbohydrate: 15 g*
Fat: 14 g   *Cholesterol: 40 mg*   *Sodium: 683 mg*
Calcium: 410 mg   *Fiber: 1 g*   *Sugars: less than 1 g*
Sugar Alcohol: 0 g

Food Exchanges: 1½ medium fat meat, 1 bread, ½ fat

■ ■ ■

5-Minute Quesadilla Breakfast
Net Carbs: 10 g

2 (8 inch) low-carb whole wheat tortillas
2 tablespoons reduced-fat cream cheese (Neufchatel)
1 tablespoon light sugar-free orange marmalade or other fruit
   spread

1. Preheat oven or toaster oven to 400°. On each tortilla, spread 1 tablespoon cream cheese almost to edges. Spread marmalade on top of cream cheese. Fold each tortilla in half. Heat in oven 3 to 4 minutes or until cream cheese begins to melt.

Yield: 2 servings   *Serving size: 1 tortilla*
Calories: 156   *Protein: 7 g*   *Carbohydrate: 21 g*
Fat: 6 g   *Cholesterol: 10 mg*   *Sodium: 390 mg*
Calcium: 10 mg   *Fiber: 11 g*   *Sugars: less than 1 g*
Sugar Alcohol: 0 g   *Food Exchanges: 1½ bread, 1½ other carb, 1 fat*

Southwest Breakfast Wrap
Net Carbs: 5 g

½ cup southwestern-style Egg Beaters® egg substitute
2 (8 inch) low-carb whole wheat tortillas
¼ cup shredded reduced-fat cheddar cheese
2 teaspoons chunky salsa

1. In non-stick skillet, scramble egg substitute according to package directions. Spread ½ scrambled eggs on each tortilla. Top with cheese and salsa. Roll up, heat in microwave 10 to 15 seconds and serve immediately.

Yield: 2 servings   *Serving size: 1 wrap*
Calories: 192   *Protein: 17 g*   *Carbohydrate: 8 g*
Fat: 11 g   *Cholesterol: 20 mg*   *Sodium: 579 mg*
Calcium: 223 mg   *Fiber: 3 g*   *Sugars: less than 1 g*
Sugar Alcohol: 0 g   *Food Exchanges: 1 fat, ½ bread, ½ medium fat meat*

Whole Wheat Banana Pancakes

Net Carbs: 21 g

1 cup whole wheat pancake mix
¼ cup Egg Beaters® egg substitute
½ banana, mashed
2 teaspoons canola oil

1. Combine all ingredients. Add 1 cup water and mix well. Preheat sprayed non-stick skillet over medium heat until water droplets sizzle and bounce.

2. Spoon 2 tablespoons pancake batter into skillet for each pancake. Cook until pancake browns on each side. Remove each batch and keep warm until serving time.

Optional: Serve with sugar-free breakfast syrup or Maple Syrup Stir-Fry Apples (p. 222).

Yield: About 10 to 12 (3 inch) pancakes   *Serving size: 2 pancakes*

Calories: 131   *Protein: 5 g*   *Carbohydrate: 24 g*
Fat: 2 g   *Cholesterol: 0 mg*   *Sodium: 519 mg*
Calcium: 53 mg   *Fiber: 3 g*   *Sugars: 5 g*
Sugar Alcohol: 0 g

Food Exchanges: 1½ bread, 1½ fruit, ½ fat

■ ■ ■

҉ Wide-Awake Wrap

Net Carbs: 5 g

½ cup Egg Beaters® egg substitute
2 (8 inch) low-carb whole wheat tortillas
2 slices turkey bacon, cooked, crumbled
¼ cup shredded reduced-fat cheddar cheese

1. In sprayed skillet over medium heat, scramble egg substitute according to package directions.

2. On each tortilla, spread ½ scrambled eggs and ½ crumbled bacon. Sprinkle with cheese. Roll up and heat in microwave 10 to 15 seconds. Serve immediately.

Yield: 2 servings   *Serving size: 1 wrap*

Calories: 221   *Protein: 19 g*   *Carbohydrate: 8 g*
Fat: 14 g   *Cholesterol: 30 mg*   *Sodium: 757 mg*
Calcium: 222 mg   *Fiber: 3 g*   *Sugars: less than 1 g*
Sugar Alcohol: 0 g

Food Exchanges: 1½ fat, 1 medium fat meat, ½ bread

■ ■ ■

Buttery Cinnamon Toast

Net Carbs: 9 g

4 slices sugar-free whole wheat bread
4 teaspoons Smart Balance® buttery spread
1 tablespoon Splenda® sugar substitute
½ tablespoon ground cinnamon

1. Toast bread. Spread each slice with 1 teaspoon buttery spread. In small bowl, combine sugar substitute and cinnamon. Sprinkle over warm toast. Serve immediately.

Yield: 4 servings   *Serving size: 1 slice*

Calories: 77   *Protein: 3 g*   *Carbohydrate: 12 g*
Fat: 2 g   *Cholesterol: 0 mg*   *Sodium: 149 mg*
Calcium: 14 mg   *Fiber: 3 g*   *Sugars: less than 1 g*
Sugar Alcohol: 0 g

Food Exchanges: ½ bread, ½ fat

■ ■ ■

Deluxe Breakfast Toast

Net Carbs: 9 g

1 tablespoon Splenda® sugar substitute
¼ teaspoon ground cinnamon
2 slices reduced-calorie or sugar-free whole wheat bread
¼ cup low-fat cottage cheese, drained, divided

1. In small bowl, mix sugar substitute and cinnamon and set aside. Lightly toast bread, then spread each slice with half cottage cheese. Sprinkle tops with cinnamon mixture.

2. Place toast under heated broiler for 1 to 2 minutes or until hot. Serve immediately.

Yield: 2 servings   *Serving size: 1 slice toast*

Calories: 67   *Protein: 6 g*   *Carbohydrate: 12 g*
Fat: less than 1 g   *Cholesterol: 1 mg* *Sodium: 232 mg*
Calcium: 39 mg   *Fiber: 3 g*   *Sugars: 1 g*
Sugar Alcohol: 0 g

Food Exchanges: 1 bread, ½ lean meat

■ ■ ■

❧ French Toast Sticks

Net Carbs: 10 g

4 slices sugar-free whole wheat bread
½ cup Egg Beaters® egg substitute
1 tablespoon Splenda® sugar substitute
½ tablespoon cinnamon

1. Preheat non-stick skillet over high heat.

2. Cut each slice bread into 3 sticks.

3. Pour egg substitute into shallow dish. In batches, coat bread sticks on both sides with egg substitute and place immediately in skillet.

4. Cook bread on both sides until it browns. Remove and place on serving plate.

5. In small bowl, combine sugar substitute and cinnamon. Sprinkle over warm toast and serve immediately.

Optional: To reduce carbs, prepare with low-carb wheat bread.

Yield: 4 servings (12 sticks) Serving size: 3 sticks

Calories: 85	*Protein: 6 g*	*Carbohydrate: 13 g*
Fat: 1 g	*Cholesterol: 0 mg*	*Sodium: 172 mg*
Calcium: 21 mg	*Fiber: 3 mg*	*Sugars: less than 1 g*
Sugar Alcohol: 0 g	*Food Exchanges: 1 bread, ½ lean meat*	

One ounce cornflakes has more sodium than 1 ounce salted peanuts.

English Muffin Breakfast
Net Carbs: 19 g

1 whole wheat English muffin halved
4 tablespoons low-fat small curd cottage cheese, well drained or
    part-skim ricotta cheese
½ cup unsweetened applesauce
½ to 1 teaspoon ground cinnamon

1. Lightly toast muffin halves.

2. Top with cottage cheese and applesauce and sprinkle with cinnamon.

3. Broil 2 to 3 minutes until cheese and applesauce heat through.

4. Serve immediately.

Optional: To reduce carbs, substitute 1 or 2 (8 inch) low-carb tortillas for English muffin.

Yield: 2 servings   Serving size: 1 muffin half

Calories: 120   Protein: 7 g   Carbohydrate: 22 g
Fat: 1 g   Cholesterol: 2 mg   Sodium: 327 mg
Calcium: 114 mg   Fiber: 3 g   Sugars: 9 g
Sugar Alcohol: 0 g

Food Exchanges: 1 bread, ½ fruit, ½ lean meat

■ ■ ■

Pesto Toasts

Net Carbs: 13 g

1 small loaf French bread (baguette)
Lower-Fat Pesto Spread (p. 208)
4 tablespoons finely shredded parmesan or romano cheese
(optional)

1. Preheat oven broiler. Slice bread ½-inch thick and toast bread on both sides until golden brown.

2. Spread each slice with 1 teaspoon pesto spread and top with 1 teaspoon parmesan cheese, if desired. Serve immediately.

Yield: 4 servings   *Serving size: 1 slice*

Calories: 87   *Protein: 3 g*   *Carbohydrate: 13 g*
Fat: 2 g   *Cholesterol: 1 mg*   *Sodium: 171 mg*
Calcium: 41 mg   *Fiber: less than 1 g* *Sugars: less than 1 g*
Sugar Alcohol: 0 g

Food Exchanges: 1 bread, ½ fat, ½ lean meat

■ ■ ■

Party Bruschetta
Net Carbs: 4 g

Bruschetta derives from an Italian word meaning "to roast over coals". It is a simple, delicious appetizer or can be used as a bread accompaniment to Italian dishes.

4 (½ -inch) thick diagonal slices French bread or baguette
1 garlic clove, cut
2 tablespoons extra-virgin olive oil
½ cup chopped, drained Roma tomatoes

1. Preheat broiler. Toast bread slices on both sides until they brown lightly. Rub each slice gently with garlic clove and drizzle each with about 2 teaspoons oil.

2. To serve, spoon 1 tablespoon tomatoes on each slice. Season to taste with black pepper and salt or salt substitute. Serve warm.

Yield: 4 servings   *Serving size: 1 slice*

Calories: 131   *Protein: 2 g*   *Carbohydrate: 4 g*
Fat: 8 g   *Cholesterol: 0 mg*   *Sodium: 153 mg*
Calcium: 20 mg   *Fiber: less than 1 g*   *Sugars: less than 1 g*
Sugar Alcohol: 0 g

Food Exchanges: 1 bread, 2 fat

■ ■ ■

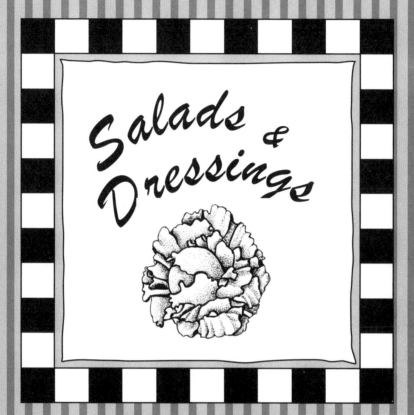

Salads & Dressings

Apple-Zucchini Green Salad
Net Carbs: 10 g

6 cups torn green or red leaf lettuce
2 cups unpeeled, cored, coarsely chopped red apple
1 cup unpeeled thinly sliced zucchini
2 to 3 tablespoons Green Salad Vinaigrette (p. 103) or olive oil
  and vinegar

1. In salad bowl, toss lettuce, apple and zucchini.

2. Drizzle vinaigrette over salad and lightly toss. Serve immediately.

Yield: 6 servings   *Serving size: 1 cup*

Calories: 57   *Protein: 2 g*   *Carbohydrate: 13 g*
Fat: less than 1 g   *Cholesterol: 0 mg*   *Sodium: 6 mg*
Calcium: 31 mg   *Fiber: 3 g*   *Sugars: 9 g*
Sugar Alcohol: 0 g

Food Exchanges: 1 fruit, ½ vegetable

■ ■ ■

Orange Red-Onion Salad

Net Carbs: 7 g

2 large navel oranges, peeled, sliced
8 thin red onion slices
6 cups bite-size romaine or leaf lettuce
4 to 5 tablespoons vinaigrette dressing

1. Quarter orange slices and place in salad bowl with red onion and lettuce.

2. Toss with vinaigrette and serve immediately.

Yield: 6 servings   *Serving size: 1 cup*

Calories (without dressing): 40   *Protein: 1 g*   *Carbohydrate: 10 g*
Fat: less than 1 g   *Cholesterol: 0 mg*   *Sodium: 5.3 mg*
Calcium: 44 mg   *Dietary Fiber: 3 g*   *Sugars: 6 g*
Sugar Alcohol: 0 g

Avocado-Grapefruit Salad
Net Carbs: 7 g

4 cups shredded romaine or leaf lettuce
1 avocado, peeled, seeded
1 grapefruit, peeled, sectioned
2 to 3 tablespoons vinaigrette dressing

1. On each of 4 salad plates, place 1 cup shredded lettuce. Slice avocado in ¼-inch wedges.

2. Arrange wedges and grapefruit sections on lettuce. Drizzle with dressing and serve immediately.

Tip: One head of lettuce yields about 8 cups shredded lettuce.

Yield: 4 servings   *Serving size: 1 individual salad*

Calories (without dressing): 106   *Protein: 2 g*   *Carbohydrate: 12 g*
Fat: 7 g   *Cholesterol: 0 mg*   *Sodium: 8 mg*
Calcium: 38 mg   *Fiber: 5 g*   *Sugar: 5 g*
Sugar Alcohol: 0 g

Food Exchanges: 1½ fat, ½ vegetable, ½ fruit

■ ■ ■

5-Minute Italian Green Salad

Net Carbs: 2 g

½ (16 ounce) jar Italian mix giardiniera (cauliflower, carrots, celery, peppers and pickles in vinegar)
1 (10 ounce) package ready-to-eat romaine lettuce
3 to 4 tablespoons Green Salad Vinaigrette (p. 103)

1. In wire mesh strainer, drain and rinse Italian mix vegetables to remove excess salt. Chill remaining vegetables in jar for later use.

2. In salad bowl, lightly toss lettuce and vegetables. Drizzle with dressing.

Tip: Prepared ready-to-eat romaine lettuce will make this recipe a snap! In 1 (10 ounce) package of ready-to-eat romaine lettuce, there are 6 to 8 cups.

Yield: 6 to 8 servings   *Serving size: 1 cup*

Calories (without dressing): 16   *Protein: less than 1 g*   *Carbohydrate: 3 g*
Fat: less than 1 g   *Cholesterol: 0 mg*   *Sodium: 368 mg*
Calcium: 22 mg   *Fiber: 1 g*   *Sugars: less than 1 g*
Sugar Alcohol: 0 g

Food Exchanges: 0

■ ■ ■

❧ Pear and Feta Cheese Salad

Net Carbs: 11 g

4 cups mixed field greens or bite-size romaine lettuce
2 Anjou pears, unpeeled, cut in large chunks
2 tablespoons crumbled feta or gorgonzola cheese
2 to 3 tablespoons Balsamic Vinaigrette (p. 99)

1. On each of 4 salad plates, place 1 cup greens.

2. Arrange ½ cup pears over greens on each plate and sprinkle feta cheese on top.

3. Drizzle with Balsamic Vinaigrette and serve immediately.

Optional: Sprinkle each salad with 1 tablespoon chopped walnuts or pecans.

Yield: 4 servings
Calories (without dressing): 70
Fat: 1 g
Calcium: 44 mg
Sugar Alcohol: 0 g
Food Exchanges: 1 fruit, ½ vegetable

Serving size: 1 cup
Protein: 2 g
Cholesterol: 4 mg
Dietary Fiber: 4 g

Carbohydrate: 15 g
Sodium: 62 mg
Sugars: 9 g

Keeping Lettuce Crisp

You will want plenty of lettuce or other greens ready at a moment's notice. Washing and storing lettuce properly will make a big difference in how long it will stay salad-fresh. Remove any bruised, wilted or brown-edged pieces. Separate leaves and wash under cold running water. Use a salad spinner to dry the lettuce, breaking large pieces to fit in the spinner. Layer dry leaves between paper towels and store in zippered plastic bag. Should keep 5 to 7 days. When ready to serve green salad, tear your fresh lettuce and toss with ingredients at the last minute.

Cottage Cheese Scramble
Net Carbs: 5 g

1 (16 ounce) carton low-fat small curd cottage cheese, drained
¼ cup chopped bell pepper
½ cup chopped fresh tomato, drained
2 tablespoons chopped green onion with tops

1. In bowl, mix all ingredients. Season to taste with black pepper and salt or salt substitute.

Tip: Garnish with chopped parsley.

Yield: 4 servings   *Serving size: ½ cup*

Calories: 85   *Protein: 14 g*   *Carbohydrate: 5 g*
Fat: 1 g   *Cholesterol: 4 mg*   *Sodium: 434 mg*
Calcium: 71 mg   *Fiber: less than 1 g*   *Sugars: 4 g*
Sugar Alcohol: 0 g

Food Exchanges: 2 very lean meat, ½ vegetable

■ ■ ■

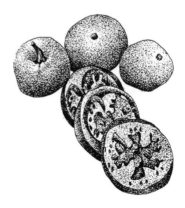

Warm Field Greens Salad

Net Carbs: 1 g

1 (10 ounce) package fresh mixed field greens or spinach
¼ cup chopped green onions with tops
2 hard-boiled egg whites, chopped
Sweet-Sour Salad Dressing (p. 101)

1. In salad bowl, combine greens, green onions and egg whites. In small saucepan, heat salad dressing until it boils. Immediately pour over salad and toss.

Optional: Add 2 tablespoons crumbled feta or gorgonzola cheese.

Yield: 4 servings   *Serving size: 1 cup*

Calories (without dressing): 23   *Protein: 3 g*   *Carbohydrate: 3 g*
Fat: less than 1 g   *Cholesterol: 0 mg*   *Sodium: 41 mg*
Calcium: 22 mg   *Fiber: 2 g*   *Sugars: 1 g*
Sugar Alcohol: 0 g

Food Exchanges: ½ very lean meat

■ ■ ■

Baby Spinach-Pecan Salad
Net Carbs: 0 g

¼ cup chopped pecans
1 (6 ounce) package ready-to-eat baby spinach
3 to 4 green onions with tops, chopped
2 tablespoons Honey-Mustard Dressing

1. In small skillet over medium heat, stir and toast pecans.

2. In salad bowl, combine spinach and green onions. Drizzle with dressing and toss lightly to coat.

3. Sprinkle salad with toasted pecans and serve immediately.

Yield: 4 servings　　　　　*Serving size: 1 cup*

Calories (with dressing): 137　　　　　*Protein: 3 g*
　Carbohydrate: 4 g
Fat: 14 g　　　*Cholesterol: 0 mg*　　*Sodium: 79 mg*
Calcium: 52 mg　　*Fiber: 5 g*　　　*Sugars: 1 g*
Sugar Alcohol: 0 g

Food Exchanges: 1 vegetable, 3 fat

Honey-Mustard Dressing

¼ cup canola oil
3 tablespoons cider vinegar
1½ tablespoons dijon-style mustard
2 teaspoons honey

1. Combine all ingredients and mix well.

Yield: 4 servings (about ½ cup)　　　*Serving size: 2 tablespoons*

■ ■ ■

Tomorrow's Layered Salad
Net Carbs: 4 g

1 head iceberg lettuce, shredded
1 cup sliced celery
1 cup frozen green peas, partially thawed
¾ cup light mayonnaise

1. In large salad bowl, layer lettuce, celery and peas.
   Spread mayonnaise to cover and seal top of salad.

2. Cover tightly and chill several hours or until next day.
   Do not toss.

Yield: 6 servings (6 to 8 cups)   *Serving size: 1 cup*

Calories: 110   *Protein: 2 g*   *Carbohydrate: 6 g*
Fat: 9 g   *Cholesterol: 9 mg*   *Sodium: 244 mg*
Calcium: 22 mg   *Fiber: 2 g*   *Sugars: 2 g*
Sugar Alcohol: 0 g

Food Exchanges: 2 fat, ½ vegetable

■ ■ ■

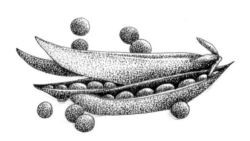

Creamy Cabbage Slaw

Net Carbs: 2 g

6 cups shredded green cabbage
¼ cup chopped green bell pepper
¼ cup sliced green onions with tops
⅓ cup Creamy Slaw Dressing (p. 102)

1. In salad bowl, combine cabbage, bell pepper and green onion. Cover and chill.

2. Just before serving, lightly toss cabbage mixture with dressing and serve immediately.

Yield: 6 to 8 servings　　*Serving size: ¾ cup*

Calories (without dressing): 17　　*Protein: less than 1 g*　　*Carbohydrate: 4 g*
Fat: less than 1 g　　*Cholesterol: 0 mg*　　*Sodium: 12 mg*
Calcium: 31 mg　　*Fiber: 2 g*　　*Sugar: 2 g*
Sugar Alcohol: 0 g

Food Exchanges: 0

Fancy Carrot Salad
Net Carbs: 7 g

3 carrots, peeled, coarsely grated
1 (8 ounce) can crushed pineapple, well drained
4 tablespoons chopped pecans
2 to 3 tablespoons light or fat-free mayonnaise

1. In salad bowl, combine all ingredients.

2. Chill before serving.

Yield: 6 to 8 servings   *Serving size: ½ cup*

Calories: 63   *Protein: less than 1 g*   *Carbohydrate: 8 g*
Fat: 3 g   *Cholesterol: 0 mg*   *Sodium: 58 mg*
Calcium: 11 mg   *Fiber: 1 g*   *Sugars: 5 g*
Sugar Alcohol: 0 g

Food Exchanges: ½ fruit, ½ fat

■ ■ ■

Fiesta Corn Salad

Net Carbs: 9 g

**1 (11 ounce) can corn with sweet red and green peppers, drained,
  rinsed**
1 cup low-fat small curd cottage cheese, drained
⅓ cup chopped green onions with tops
⅓ cup light sour cream

1. In mixing bowl, combine corn, cottage cheese and green
   onions. If needed, strain mixture again to remove excess
   liquid.

2. Stir in sour cream.

3. Cover and chill before serving.

Yield: 6 to 8 servings   *Serving size: ½ cup*

Calories: 81   *Protein: 5 g*   *Carbohydrate: 10 g*
Fat: 3 g   *Cholesterol: 9 mg*   *Sodium: 281 mg*
Calcium: 35 mg   *Fiber: 1 g*   *Sugars: 2 g*
Sugar Alcohol: 0 g

Food Exchanges: ½ milk, ½ fat

■ ■ ■

Black Bean-Corn Salad

Net Carbs: 19 g

1 (15½ ounce) can black beans, drained, rinsed
1 cup frozen corn kernels, thawed
½ cup diced tomatoes, drained
6 green onions with tops, sliced

1. In large bowl, combine all ingredients. Season to taste with black pepper and salt or salt substitute.

2. Cover and chill at least 1 hour before serving.

Tip: Sprinkle each serving with lime juice and fresh chopped cilantro.

Yield: 4 servings   *Serving size: ½ cup*

Calories: 106   *Protein: 6 g*   *Carbohydrate: 25 g*
Fat: 0 g   *Cholesterol: 0 mg*   *Sodium: 282 mg*
Calcium: 66 mg   *Fiber: 6 g*   *Sugars: 4 g*
Sugar Alcohol: 0 g

Food Exchanges: 1 bread, ½ vegetable

■ ■ ■

Crunchy Veggie Salad
Net Carbs: 2 g

½ cup sliced radishes
½ cup sliced celery
1 cup sliced zucchini
2 to 3 tablespoons Classic French Dressing (p. 97) or oil and
    vinegar

1. In salad bowl, mix radishes, celery and zucchini and chill.

2. Just before serving, drizzle salad with dressing and lightly toss.

Yield: 4 servings   *Serving size: ½ cup*

Calories (without dressing): 19   *Protein: 2 g*   *Carbohydrate: 3 g*
Fat: less than 1 g   *Cholesterol: 0 mg*   *Sodium: 30 mg*
Calcium: 27 mg   *Fiber: 1 g*   *Sugars: 2 g*
Sugar Alcohol: 0 g

Food Exchanges: 0

■ ■ ■

Warm Three-Bean Salad

Net Carbs: 0 g

2 (15 ounce) cans three-bean salad
1 (8 ounce) can sliced water chestnuts
Sweet-Sour Salad Dressing (p. 101)
2 tablespoons bacon bits

1. Drain cans of three-bean salad and water chestnuts and rinse thoroughly in cold water to remove excess sodium. Place in large ovenproof bowl.

2. Heat Sweet-Sour Salad Dressing (p. 101) and pour over bean mixture. Sprinkle bacon bits on top (do not stir). Serve immediately.

Yield: 6 servings (about 3 cups)   *Serving size: ½ cup*

Calories (without dressing): 134   *Protein: 3 g*   *Carbohydrate: 5 g*
Fat: less than 1 g   *Cholesterol: 26 mg*   *Sodium: 546 mg*
Calcium: 1 mg   *Fiber: 5 g*   *Sugars: 18 mg*
Sugar Alcohol: 0 g

Food Exchanges: 0

■ ■ ■

Baby Pea Salad
Net Carbs: 5 g

1 (16 ounce) package frozen petite peas
1 cup thinly sliced celery
¼ cup finely chopped green onions with tops
⅓ cup Tangy Basil Dressing (p. 104)

1. Cook peas according to package directions. Do not overcook. Drain and cool slightly. In salad bowl, combine all ingredients. Chill several hours or overnight, stirring occasionally. Drain excess dressing when ready to serve.

Variation: Substitute 1 (15 ounce) can petite peas, drained, for frozen peas.

Yield: 8 servings   *Serving size: ½ cup*

Calories (without dressing): 47   *Protein: 3 g*   *Carbohydrate: 8 g*
Fat: less than 1 g   *Cholesterol: 0 mg*   *Sodium: 75 mg*
Calcium: 6 mg   *Fiber: 3 g*   *Sugars: 4 g*
Sugar Alcohol: 0 g

Food Exchanges: ½ vegetable

■ ■ ■

Greek Salad
Net Carbs: 3 g

2 large tomatoes, cut into wedges
⅓ cup red onion slivers
8 large pitted black olives, sliced
2 to 3 tablespoons Feta Cheese Dressing, (p. 98)

1. In salad bowl, combine tomatoes, red onions and olives. Toss with dressing and serve immediately.

Yield: 6 servings (about 3 cups)   *Serving size: ½ cup*

Calories (without dressing): 18   *Protein: less than 1 g*   *Carbohydrate: 3 g*
Fat: less than 1 g   *Cholesterol: 0 mg*   *Sodium: 55 mg*
Calcium: 8 mg   *Fiber: less than 1 g*   *Sugars: less than 1 g*
Sugar Alcohol: 0 g

Food Exchanges: 0

■ ■ ■

Italian Green Bean Salad

Net Carbs: 5 g

1 (16 ounce) package frozen cut Italian green beans or regular cut
   green beans
2 tablespoons canned diced pimento or diced roasted red pepper
2 tablespoons grated parmesan or romano cheese
⅓ cup light mayonnaise

1. Cook green beans according to package directions and drain. Do not overcook.

2. In salad bowl, mix all ingredients. Serve warm or chilled.

Variation: Substitute 4 cups canned cut Italian green beans, drained, rinsed for frozen green beans.

Yield: 8 servings (about 4 cups)   *Serving size: ½ cup*

Calories: 88	*Protein: 1 g*	*Carbohydrate: 7 g*
Fat: 7 g	*Cholesterol: 8 mg*	*Sodium: 143 mg*
Calcium: 42 mg	*Fiber: 2 g*	*Sugars: 2 g*
Sugar Alcohol: 0 g		

Food Exchanges: 1½ fat, ½ vegetable

■ ■ ■

Cauliflower-Olive Salad

Net Carbs: 1 g

1 (12 ounce) head raw cauliflower
¼ cup sliced black olives, drained
¼ cup diced pimentos, drained
2 to 3 tablespoons Classic French Dressing (p. 97) or oil and'
    vinegar

1. Wash cauliflower and remove leaves and woody stems. Separate cauliflower into florets.

2. Transfer florets to small saucepan and cover with about 1 inch water. Cover and boil 8 to 10 minutes or until cauliflower is crisp tender. (To cook in microwave, place raw florets in covered dish with 2 tablespoons water. Cook on HIGH for 5 to 6 minutes or just until cauliflower is crisp tender.)

3. Drain cooked florets and cool 10 to 15 minutes.

4. In salad bowl, mix cauliflower, olives and pimentos. Toss lightly with 2 to 3 tablespoons Classic French Dressing. Season to taste with salt substitute and pepper.

5. Serve on lettuce leaf or toss with salad greens.

Tip: One head cauliflower yields about 3 cups florets.

Yield: *6 servings (About 3 ½ cups)*   Serving size: *½ cup*

Calories *(without dressing)*: *21*   Protein: *1 g*   Carbohydrate: *3 g*
Fat: *less than 1 g*   Cholesterol: *0 mg*   Sodium: *66 mg*
Calcium: *17 mg*   Dietary Fiber: *2 g*   Sugars: *1 g*
Sugar Alcohol: *0 g*

Food Exchanges: *0*

Artichoke-Red Pepper Salad

Net Carbs: 3 g

1 (6 ounce) jar marinated artichoke hearts
½ cup slivered red bell pepper
¼ cup slivered white or yellow onion
1 head torn romaine lettuce or torn fresh spinach

1. Drain artichoke hearts and reserve marinade.

2. Coarsely chop artichoke hearts and place in mixing bowl. Add red bell pepper and onions.

3. Add 2 tablespoons reserved marinade and stir. Cover and chill.

4. Place lettuce in salad bowl and add marinated vegetables. Toss to lightly coat lettuce. Serve immediately.

Optional: You may substitute green bell pepper for red bell pepper. You may substitute canned roasted red pepper or ¼ cup drained sliced pimentos for the fresh bell pepper.

Yield: 8 servings   *Serving size: 1 cup*

Calories: 47   *Protein: less than 1 g*   *Carbohydrate: 4 g*
Fat: 4 g   *Cholesterol: 0 mg*   *Sodium: 78 mg*
Calcium: 20 mg   *Fiber: 1 g*   *Sugars: 1 g*
Sugar Alcohol: 0 g

Food Exchanges: 1 fat

If your lettuce or greens have passed the peak of freshness, they will still taste great when cooked as wilted.

Easy Spanish Slaw
Net Carbs: 3 g

1 tablespoon canola or olive oil
1 tablespoon apple cider vinegar
3 cups shredded cabbage or ready-to-eat coleslaw mix
½ cup slivered bell pepper

1. In bowl, mix oil and vinegar.

2. In salad bowl, pour oil-vinegar mixture over cabbage and bell pepper and gently toss. (Chop or shred any large cabbage pieces in coleslaw mix before using.)

3. Cover and chill at least 15 minutes before serving.

Tip: For a sweeter taste, add ½ teaspoon sugar substitute to oil-vinegar mixture.

Yield: 3 servings   Serving size: 1 cup

Calories: 61   Protein: 1 g   Carbohydrate: 5 g
Fat: 5 g   Cholesterol: 0 mg   Sodium: 13 mg
Calcium: 35 mg   Fiber: 2 g   Sugars: 3 g
Sugar Alcohol: 0 g

Food Exchanges: 1 fat, 1 vegetable

■ ■ ■

Tabbouleh Slaw

Net Carbs: 16 g

1 (5.25 ounce) package tabbouleh wheat salad mix, divided
1 tablespoon fresh lemon juice
1 tablespoon olive oil
2 cups packaged broccoli-slaw mix (broccoli, carrots, red cabbage)

1. In large bowl, combine dry tabbouleh mix and seasoning packet. Add 1 cup boiling water and mix well. Cover and chill 30 minutes.

2. After chilling, stir in lemon juice and oil. Reserve 1 cup prepared tabbouleh. (Store remaining tabbouleh for use in another salad recipe.)

3. Just before serving, combine 1 cup reserved tabbouleh with 2 cups broccoli-slaw mix and toss.

Yield: 4 servings   *Serving size: 1 cup*

Calories: 119   *Protein: 4 g*   *Carbohydrate: 21 g*
Fat: 3 g   *Cholesterol: 0 mg*   *Sodium: 249 mg*
Calcium: less than 1 g *Fiber: 5 g*   *Sugars: 2 g*
Sugar Alcohol: 0 g

Food Exchanges: 1 bread, 1 vegetable

■ ■ ■

⅛ Oriental Chicken Slaw
Net Carbs: 14 g

1 (3 ounce) package ramen noodles, crushed
½ cup diced cooked chicken breast
4 cups shredded cabbage or coleslaw mix
2 to 3 tablespoons Sesame Seed Dressing (p. 100) or oil and
  vinegar

1. In dry skillet over medium heat, cook and stir noodles until they turn light brown. Stir constantly to avoid burning.

2. In salad bowl, combine toasted noodles, chicken and cabbage.

3. Drizzle with 2 tablespoons Sesame Seed Dressing. Toss lightly and serve immediately.

Yield: 4 servings   *Serving size: 1½ cups*

Calories (without dressing): 140   *Protein: 8 g*   *Carbohydrate: 16 g*
Fat: 5 g   *Cholesterol: 12 mg*   *Sodium: 549 mg*
Calcium: 33 mg   *Fiber: 2 g*   *Sugars: 3 g*
Sugar Alcohol: 0 g

Food Exchanges: 1 bread, ½ meat, ½ vegetable

■ ■ ■

Chicken-Pasta Salad

Net Carbs: 17 g

1 (16 to 20 ounce) package frozen vegetable blend
1½ cups cooked reduced-carb pasta
2 broiled boneless, skinless chicken breasts, cubed
2 to 3 teaspoons Sesame Seed Dressing (p. 100)

1. Cook vegetables according to package directions.
   Do not overcook. Drain. In salad bowl, combine all
   ingredients and lightly toss. Season to taste with salt
   substitute and pepper.

*Tip: The vegetable blend with mushrooms, broccoli and
squash is really good. Try rotini, shells or macaroni for
pasta.*

Yield: 4 servings   *Serving size: ½ to ¾ cup*

Calories (without dressing): 234   *Protein: 26 g*   *Carbohydrate: 26 g*
Fat: 2 g   *Cholesterol: 43 mg*   *Sodium: 312 mg*
Calcium: 28 mg   *Fiber: 9 g*   *Sugars: 4 g*
Sugar Alcohol: 0 g

Food Exchanges: 3 bread, 2 very lean meat, 2 vegetable

■ ■ ■

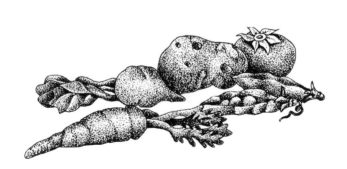

❧ Classic Tuna Salad

Net Carbs: 5 g

1 (6 ounce) can solid white albacore tuna in water
2 tablespoons light or fat-free mayonnaise
1 red apple, unpeeled, diced
½ cup diced celery

1. Drain tuna and break up with fork. Transfer to salad bowl. Add mayonnaise, apple and celery. Toss lightly to mix.

Optional: Add ¼ cup chopped pecans.

Yield: 4 servings   *Serving size: ½ cup*

Calories: 86   *Protein: 11 g*   *Carbohydrate: 6 g*
Fat: 2 g   *Cholesterol: 19 mg*   *Sodium: 269 mg*
Calcium: 12 mg   *Fiber: 1 g*   *Sugars: 4 g*
Sugar Alcohol: 0 g

Food Exchanges: 1½ lean meat, 1 fruit, 1 vegetable

■ ■ ■

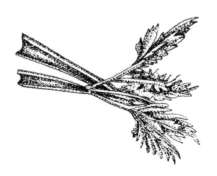

Curried Fruit and Chicken Salad

Net Carbs: 6 g

¼ teaspoon curry powder
2 tablespoons light mayonnaise, divided
2 cups diced cooked, boneless, skinless chicken breasts
1 cup seedless red or green grapes, halved

1. In mixing bowl, combine curry powder and 1
   tablespoon mayonnaise. Add chicken and grapes and
   mix. If needed to moisten ingredients, add remaining
   1 tablespoon mayonnaise.

Yield: 6 servings   *Serving size: ¼ cup*

Calories: 112   *Protein: 15 g*   *Carbohydrate: 6 g*
Fat: 3 g   *Cholesterol: 41 mg*   *Sodium: 65 mg*
Calcium: 10 mg   *Fiber: less than 1 g*   *Sugars: 4 g*
Sugar Alcohol: 0 g

Food Exchanges: ½ lean meat, ½ fruit, ½ fat

*Starchy vegetables such as corn, peas, and potatoes are
found on the starch rather than vegetable Exchange List.*

Tomato-Asparagus Salad
Net Carbs: 4 g

½ pound fresh asparagus or 1 (10 ounce) package frozen
   asparagus spears
2 tomatoes, sliced
2 cooked egg whites, chopped
2 tablespoons fat-free Italian dressing

1. Wash and trim asparagus spears. In skillet, heat 1 inch water until it boils. Cook asparagus in boiling water 5 minutes or just until it is crisp-tender and drain. Follow package directions to cook asparagus.

2. Divide tomato slices evenly among 4 saucers. Divide cooked asparagus spears evenly and place on top of tomatoes. Sprinkle each salad with ¼ cooked egg white and top with 2 teaspoons dressing.

Yield: 4 servings

Serving size: 1 salad (3 to 4 tomato slices, 3 to 4 asparagus spears, 1 tablespoon egg white and 2 teaspoons salad dressing)

Calories: 39
Fat: less than 1 g
Calcium: 21 mg
Sugar Alcohol: 0 g

Protein: 4 g
Cholesterol: 0 mg
Fiber: 2 g

Carbohydrate: 6 g
Sodium: 122 mg
Sugars: 3 g

Food Exchanges: 2 vegetable

■ ■ ■

Tuna Salad Tomato Cups
Net Carbs: 5 g

3 large firm ripe tomatoes
1 (6 ounce) can solid white albacore tuna in water, drained
⅓ cup light mayonnaise
½ cup chopped celery

1. Cut off about ⅓ of stem end of each tomato. Carefully scoop out tomato pulp and save for later use or discard.

2. In mixing bowl, mix tuna, mayonnaise and celery. Season to taste with salt substitute and pepper. Mound ⅓ tuna mixture in each tomato cup and serve.

Optional: Add 1 tablespoon dill or sweet pickle relish to tuna mixture.

Yield: 3 servings   *Serving size: 1 tomato cup*

Calories: 182   *Protein: 16 g*   *Carbohydrate: 7 g*
Fat: 10 g   *Cholesterol: 34 mg*   *Sodium: 478 mg*
Calcium: 21 mg   *Fiber: 2 g*   *Sugars: 3 g*
Sugar Alcohol: 0 g

Food Exchanges: 2 medium fat meat, 1 other carb, ½ vegetable

On-the-Go Shrimp Salad
Net Carbs: 2 g

4 cups shredded iceberg lettuce
1 large firm ripe tomato
½ pound frozen cooked shrimp, thawed
2 to 4 tablespoons Lemon Oil Dressing (p. 215) or oil and vinegar

1. On each of 4 salad plates, place 1 cup lettuce. Top
   with tomato wedges and shrimp. Drizzle 1 tablespoon
   dressing on each. Serve immediately.

Tip: *You could also use 2 to 3 Roma (pear) tomatoes, cut in*
wedges.

Yield: *4 servings*   *Serving size:* *1½ cups*

Calories (without dressing)*:* 67   *Protein: 13 g*   *Carbohydrate: 2 g*
Fat: *less than 1 g*   *Cholesterol: 111 mg*   *Sodium: 133 mg*
Calcium: 36 mg   *Fiber: less than 1 g*   *Sugars: 2 g*
Sugar Alcohol: 0 g

Food Exchanges: *½ very lean meat*

■ ■ ■

Potluck Peach Salad

Net Carbs: 8 g

2 (.3 ounce) packages sugar-free peach gelatin mix
1 (20 ounce) can pineapple tidbits and juice
2 red apples, unpeeled, cored, diced
½ cup chopped pecans

1. In saucepan, heat 2 cups water until it boils. Add gelatin and stir until it dissolves.

2. Combine pineapple juice only and enough water to equal
   1 cup. Stir into dissolved gelatin.

3. Pour mixture into 9 x 13-inch dish and chill until it begins to thicken.

4. Stir in pineapple, apples and pecans and chill until gelatin sets.

Optional: Serve with reduced-fat or fat-free whipped topping.

Yield: 12 to 14 servings   *Serving size: ½ cup*

Calories: 64   *Protein: less than 1 g*   *Carbohydrate: 9 g*
Fat: 3 g   *Cholesterol: 0 mg*   *Sodium: 33 mg*
Calcium: 4 mg   *Fiber: 1 g*   *Sugars: 7 g*
Sugar Alcohol: 0 g

Food Exchanges: ½ fruit, ½ fat

■ ■ ■

Green Light Gelatin
Net Carbs: 7 g

1 (.3 ounce) package sugar-free lime gelatin mix
1 (8 ounce) can crushed pineapple in juice with liquid
2 tablespoons light mayonnaise
1 cup low-fat small curd cottage cheese, drained

1. In saucepan, heat 1 cup water until it boils. Add gelatin mix and stir until it dissolves. Add crushed pineapple with juice and mayonnaise and mix. Stir in cottage cheese and mix well. Pour into 1-quart square dish and chill until gelatin sets.

Yield: 6 servings   *Serving size: About ½ cup*

Calories: 78   *Protein: 6 g*   *Carbohydrate: 7 g*
Fat: 2 g   *Cholesterol: 5 mg*   *Sodium: 227 mg*
Calcium: 26 mg   *Fiber: less than 1 g*   *Sugars: 5 g*
Sugar Alcohol: 0 g

Food Exchanges: 1 lean meat, ½ fruit, ½ other carb

■ ■ ■

Fruit canned in extra-light syrup generally has the same grams of carbohydrate per serving as does fruit canned in juice. Not so for fruit canned in heavy syrup!

⅔ Pineapple-Blueberry Gelatin Salad

Net Carbs: 7 g

2 (.3 ounce) packages sugar-free raspberry or cranberry gelatin mix
1½ cups fresh or frozen blueberries
1 (8 ounce) can crushed pineapple with juice
1 (8 ounce) carton lite whipped topping, thawed

1. In saucepan, heat 2 cups water until it boils. Add gelatin and stir until it dissolves.

2. In mixing bowl, combine blueberry syrup, pineapple juice and enough water to equal 1 cup. Stir into gelatin mixture. Set aside ½ cup gelatin mixture.

3. Add pineapple and blueberries to gelatin and mix well.

4. Pour gelatin into 9 x 13-inch dish. Chill several hours or until gelatin sets.

5. Fold ½ cup reserved gelatin mixture into 1 cup whipped topping. Lightly fold in remaining whipped topping. Spread over firm gelatin. Chill before serving.

Tip: One (15 ounce) can blueberries in light syrup with juice will also work in this recipe.

Yield: 16 servings (About 8 cups)   *Serving size: ½ cup*

Calories: 53   *Protein: less than 1 g*   *Carbohydrate: 7 g*
Fat: 2 g   *Cholesterol: 0 mg*   *Sodium: 25 mg*
Calcium: 2 mg   *Fiber: less than 1 g*   *Sugars: 5 g*
Sugar Alcohol: 0 g

Food Exchanges: 0

■ ■ ■

Perfection Gelatin Mold
Net Carbs: 2 g

2 (.3 ounce) packages sugar-free lemon gelatin mix
2 cups finely shredded or chopped green cabbage
1 cup grated carrot
1 cup chopped celery

1. In saucepan, heat 2 cups water until it boils. Stir in gelatin and stir until it dissolves. Transfer to large bowl and chill gelatin until it thickens, about 45 to 60 minutes.

2. Carefully fold remaining ingredients into thickened gelatin. Pour gelatin into sprayed 6-cup ring mold.

3. Chill until firm, about 4 hours or overnight. Remove gelatin salad from mold onto serving plate.

Yield: 12 servings   *Serving size: ½ cup*

Calories: 9   *Protein: less than 1 g*   *Carbohydrate: 2 g*
Fat: less than 1 g   *Cholesterol: 0 mg*   *Sodium: 21 mg*
Calcium: 11 mg   *Fiber: less than 1 g*   *Sugars: less than 1 g*
Sugar Alcohol: 0 g

Food Exchanges: 0

◆

A "free" food is any food or drink with 20 calories or less and 5 grams carbs or less per serving.

Classic French Dressing

Net Carbs: less than 1 g

½ cup canola, peanut, or olive oil
¼ cup white wine or rice vinegar
1 teaspoon dry mustard or dijon-style mustard
1 teaspoon ground paprika

1. Combine all ingredients in bottle or jar with lid. Season to taste with salt substitute and pepper.

2. Shake well. Shake again before serving.

Yield: 12 servings (About ¾ cup)   *Serving size: 2 teaspoons*

Calories: 83	*Protein: less than 1 g*	*Carbohydrate: less than 1 g*
Fat: 9 g	*Cholesterol: 0 mg*	*Sodium: 10 mg*
Calcium: 1 mg	*Fiber: less than 1 g*	*Sugars: less than 1 g*
Sugar Alcohol: 0 g		

Food Exchanges: 2 fat

■ ■ ■

Feta Cheese Dressing
Net Carbs: 2 g

2 tablespoons canola, peanut or olive oil
3 tablespoons balsamic vinegar, red wine vinegar or cider vinegar
1 tablespoon fresh basil or 1 teaspoon dried basil
2 tablespoons crumbled feta cheese

1. Combine all ingredients and mix well. Transfer to container with lid.

2. Shake well before using.

Yield: 6 servings (About ½ cup) Serving size: 2 teaspoons

Calories: 58	*Protein: less than 1 g*	*Carbohydrate: 2 g*
Fat: 5 g	*Cholesterol: 2 mg*	*Sodium: 33 mg*
Calcium: 8 mg	*Fiber: less than 1 g*	*Sugars: 2 g*
Sugar Alcohol: 0 g		

Food Exchanges: 1 fat

■ ■ ■

Balsamic Vinaigrette
Net Carbs: 2 g

2 tablespoons canola, peanut or olive oil
3 tablespoons dark or white balsamic vinegar
¼ teaspoon dried basil, crushed
¼ teaspoon dijon-style mustard

1. In sealed container, mix or shake all ingredients until they blend well.

2. Add ¼ teaspoon black pepper.

3. Shake again before serving.

Yield: 6 servings (about ½ cup)   *Serving size: 2 tablespoons*

Calories: 51   *Protein: 0 g*   *Carbohydrate: 2 g*
Fat: 5 g   *Cholesterol: 0 mg*   *Sodium: 6 mg*
Calcium: less than 1 mg *Fiber: 0 g*   *Sugars: 2 g*
Sugar Alcohol: 0 g

Food Exchanges: 1 fat

◆

Distilled white vinegar is made from distilled grain alcohol and has a strong, sour flavor.

Balsamic vinegar is made from white Trebbiano grape juice and aged at least ten years. The vinegar has a slight sweetness, dark brown color and syrupy body. There are a variety of balsamic vinegars now in supermarkets.

Wine vinegars are made from red or white wine and derive flavor from the type of wine used.

Sesame Seed Dressing
Net Carbs: less than 1 g

1 tablespoon sesame seeds
2 tablespoons canola, peanut or olive oil
2 tablespoons white wine or rice vinegar
1 tablespoon lite (reduced sodium) soy sauce

1. In dry skillet over medium heat, cook and stir sesame seeds until they turn light brown. Stir constantly to avoid burning.

2. In jar or bottle with lid, combine all ingredients. Shake well to blend. Shake again before serving.

Yield: About 7 servings (About ⅓ cup)   *Serving size: 2 teaspoons*

Calories: 45   *Protein: less than 1 g*   *Carbohydrate: less than 1 g*
Fat: 5 g   *Cholesterol: 0 mg*   *Sodium: 83 mg*
Calcium: 14 mg   *Fiber: less than 1 g*   *Sugars: less than 1 g*
Sugar Alcohol: 0 g

Food Exchanges: 1 fat

■ ■ ■

Sweet-Sour Salad Dressing

Net Carbs: less than 1 g

¼ cup canola oil
¼ cup white wine vinegar
2 tablespoons Splenda® sugar substitute
¼ teaspoon regular or white wine Worcestershire sauce

1. Combine ingredients and shake well before using.

Yield: 4 servings (½ cup)   *Serving size: 2 tablespoons*

Calories: 126	*Protein: 0 g*	*Carbohydrate: less than 1 g*
Fat: 14 g	*Cholesterol: 0 mg*	*Sodium: less than 1 mg*
Calcium: 1 mg	*Fiber: 0 g*	*Sugars: less than 1 g*
Sugar Alcohol: 0 g		

Food Exchanges: 3 fat

■ ■ ■

Creamy Slaw Dressing

Net Carbs: 2 g

½ cup light or fat-free mayonnaise
1 tablespoon Splenda® sugar substitute
1 tablespoons cider vinegar or rice vinegar
½ teaspoon celery seed

1. In mixing bowl, cream all ingredients and ½ teaspoon salt substitute.

2. Chill in covered container.

Optional: Add 1 to 2 additional teaspoons vinegar, if desired.

Yield: 12 servings (about ¾ cup)   *Serving size: 2 teaspoons*

Calories: 34   *Protein: less than 1 g*   *Carbohydrate: 2 g*
Fat: 3 g   *Cholesterol: 3 mg*   *Sodium: 60 mg*
Calcium: 2 mg   *Fiber: less than 1 g*   *Sugars: less than 1 g*
Sugar Alcohol: 0 g

Food Exchanges: ½ fat

Green Salad Vinaigrette
Net Carbs: less than 1 g

3 tablespoons canola, peanut or olive oil
2 tablespoons cider vinegar or red wine vinegar or lemon juice
1½ teaspoons Splenda® sugar substitute

1. In bottle or jar with lid, combine oil, vinegar and sugar substitute with ¼ teaspoon salt substitute and dash freshly ground black pepper.

2. Shake well before using.

Yield: 6 to 7 servings   *Serving size:* 2 teaspoons

Calories: 61   *Protein:* 0 g   *Carbohydrate: less than 1 g*
Fat: 7 g   *Cholesterol:* 0 mg   *Sodium: less than 1 mg*
Calcium: less than 1 mg   *Dietary Fiber:* 0 g   *Sugars: less than 1 g*
Sugar Alcohol: 0 g

Food Exchanges: 1½ fat

■ ■ ■

Tangy Basil Dressing

Net Carbs: less than 1 g

¼ cup apple cider vinegar
¼ cup Splenda® sugar substitute
¼ cup canola, peanut or olive oil
1 teaspoon crushed dried basil

1. In small saucepan over medium heat, heat vinegar and sugar substitute until it dissolves. Remove from heat.

2. Add oil, basil and ½ teaspoon salt substitute and mix well. Mix again before serving.

Variation: Substitute dried dillweed for basil.

Yield: About 12 servings (¾ cup)   *Serving: 1 to 2 teaspoons*

Calories: 41   *Protein: 0 g*   *Carbohydrate: less than 1 g*
Fat: 5 g   *Cholesterol: 0 mg*   *Sodium: less than 1 g*
Calcium: less than 1 g   *Fiber: 0 g*   *Sugars: less than 1 g*
Sugar Alcohol: 0 g

Food Exchanges: 1 fat

◆

Apple cider vinegar is made from fermented apple cider and has a strong bite with slight apple flavor.

Vegetables
& Soups

Asparagus with Garlic and Basil
Net Carbs: 3 g

1½ pounds asparagus, washed, trimmed
2 cloves garlic, minced
1 teaspoon dried crushed basil or 1 tablespoon fresh basil,
     finely chopped
1 tablespoon lite (reduced sodium) soy sauce

1. In non-stick large skillet or Dutch oven, heat ⅓ cup
    water until it boils.

2. Add asparagus, cover and cook over medium heat about
    5 minutes or until asparagus is crisp-tender. Uncover
    and continue to boil about 1 to 2 minutes until water
    evaporates. Do not overcook. Remove asparagus and
    keep warm.

3. Spray dry skillet with cooking spray and add garlic and
    basil. Cook and stir 1 to 2 minutes.

4. Stir in soy sauce and season to taste with black pepper.
    Pour sauce over cooked asparagus. Serve immediately.

Yield: 6 to 8 servings   *Serving size: ½ cup*

Calories: 26   *Protein: 3 g*   *Carbohydrate: 5 g*
Fat: less than 1 g   *Cholesterol: 0 mg*   *Sodium: 98 mg*
Calcium: 30 mg   *Fiber: 2 g*   *Sugars: 2 g*
Sugar Alcohol: 0 g

Food Exchanges: ½ vegetable

◆

*Before adding a dried herb to a recipe, crush it between your
finger and thumb to help release the herb's flavor. Add it
to a recipe at the beginning of cooking to develop flavor.*

Oriental Asparagus
Net Carbs: 2 g

1 pound fresh asparagus
2 tablespoons lite (reduced sodium) soy sauce
1 tablespoon cooking sherry
¼ teaspoon ground ginger

1. In saucepan, heat 1 inch water until it boils. Wash asparagus, remove tough ends and cut in 2-inch lengths. Add asparagus to water and cook until crisp-tender, about 4 to 5 minutes. Do not overcook. Drain and set aside.

2. Mix soy sauce, sherry and ground ginger.

3. In saucepan, combine asparagus and sauce. Cook and stir over medium heat until sauce and asparagus heat through. Serve immediately.

Variation: If you don't want to use cooking sherry, substitute 1 tablespoon Splenda® sugar substitute.

Yield: 8 servings | Serving size: ½ cup

Calories: 17	Protein: 2 g	Carbohydrate: 3 g
Fat: less than 1 g	Cholesterol: 0 mg	Sodium: 156 mg
Calcium: 17 mg	Fiber: 1 g	Sugars: 1 g
Sugar Alcohol: 0 g		

Food Exchanges: 0

We should eat 3 to 5 servings of vegetables every day. Keep plenty of raw, frozen and canned vegetables on hand so you always have vegetables ready to eat.

Beets in Sweet-Sour Sauce

Net Carbs: 7 g

1 (16 ounce) can sliced or whole beets
2 teaspoons corn starch
2 tablespoons Splenda® sugar substitute
2 tablespoons cider vinegar

1. Drain liquid from beets into measuring cup. Combine beet liquid and water to equal ½ cup and set aside.

2. Mix corn starch and sugar substitute. Stir in vinegar and mix well.

3. In saucepan over medium heat, combine corn starch mixture and beet liquid. Heat to boiling and boil 1 to 2 minutes. Stir in beets and cook until they heat through.

Yield: 4 to 6 servings   *Serving size: ½ cup*

Calories: 31   *Protein: less than 1 g*   *Carbohydrate: 8 g*
Fat: 0 g   *Cholesterol: 0 mg*   *Sodium: 214 mg*
Calcium: less than 1 mg   *Fiber: 1 g*   *Sugars: 4 g*
Sugar Alcohol: 0 g

Food Exchanges: ½ vegetable

To cut down on salt, use fresh and frozen vegetables. Drain and rinse canned vegetables, and look for "no added salt" varieties.

7-Minute Broccoli Stir-Fry
Net Carbs: 3 g

1 pound fresh broccoli florets
1 (8 ounce) package fresh mushrooms, sliced
2 green onions with tops, sliced
¼ cup slivered almonds, toasted

1. Preheat sprayed non-stick wok or skillet on high heat. When hot, add broccoli and stir fry 1 minute.

2. Add 1 tablespoon water, cover and cook, stirring frequently, about 3 minutes or until broccoli is crisp-tender. Add more water if needed. Remove broccoli and set aside.

3. Spray wok with non-stick cooking spray and add mushrooms and green onions. Cook and stir until liquid from mushrooms evaporates, about 3 minutes.

4. Return broccoli to wok, stir and heat mixture until hot. Sprinkle with almonds and serve immediately.

Yield: 6 to 8 servings	*Serving size: ¾ cup*	
Calories: 58	*Protein: 4 g*	*Carbohydrate: 5 g*
Fat: 3 g	*Cholesterol: 0 mg*	*Sodium: 18 mg*
Calcium: 32 mg	*Fiber: 2 g*	*Sugars: 2 g*
Sugar Alcohol: 0 g	*Food Exchanges: ½ vegetable, ½ fat*	

The best way to clean fresh mushrooms is to wipe them with a clean, damp cloth or use a soft mushroom brush. If you wish, lightly rinse and dry immediately. Do not soak fresh mushrooms because it will ruin their texture. To keep mushrooms firm longer, store loose mushrooms or those in an opened package in a paper bag in the refrigerator. Storing in a plastic bag causes quick deterioration.

Better Brussels Sprouts

Net Carbs: 7 g

1 (10 ounce) package frozen brussels sprouts
1 onion, chopped
1 tomato, seeded, diced, drained
4 to 5 tablespoons light or fat-free sour cream

1. Cook sprouts according to package directions. Set aside and keep warm.

2. In sprayed skillet over medium heat, cook and stir onion until tender. Stir in tomato and cook until it heats through.

3. Stir in tomato, sprouts and salt substitute and pepper to taste.

4. Garnish individual servings with 1 tablespoon sour cream.

Yield: 4 to 5 servings   *Serving size: ½ cup*

Calories: 66   *Protein: 4 g*   *Carbohydrate: 10 g*
Fat: 2 g   *Cholesterol: 6 mg*   *Sodium: 16 mg*
Calcium: 43 mg   *Fiber: 3 g*   *Sugars: 2 g*
Sugar Alcohol: 0 g

Food Exchanges: ½ vegetable, ½ fat

Vegetables contribute 1 to 4 grams of fiber per serving.

Cheesy Garlic Brussels Sprouts

Net Carbs: 7 g

½ cup Easy-to-Make Cheese Sauce (p. 212)
1 (10 ounce) package frozen brussels sprouts
1 clove garlic, finely minced
1 tablespoon fresh lemon juice

1. Prepare Easy-to-Make Cheese Sauce (p. 212). Set aside and keep warm.

2. Prepare brussels sprouts according to package directions. Drain and keep warm.

3. In sprayed non-stick skillet over low heat, cook and stir garlic 1 to 2 minutes. Add drained sprouts and lemon juice and stir 2 to 3 minutes or until sprouts heat through.

4. Top each serving with 1 tablespoon cheese sauce.

Yield: 4 servings   *Serving size: ½ cup sprouts plus 2 tablespoons sauce*

Calories: 87   *Protein: 6 g*   *Carbohydrate: 10 g*
Fat: 4 g   *Cholesterol: 11 mg*   *Sodium: 97 mg*
Calcium: 106 mg   *Fiber: 3 g*   *Sugars: 2 g*
Sugar Alcohol: 0 g

Food Exchanges: 1 vegetable, ½ milk, ½ fat

■ ■ ■

Cabbage Stir-Fry
Net Carbs: 5 g

1 large onion, thinly sliced
1 to 2 cloves garlic, finely minced
1 small head (about 1¼ pounds) green cabbage, shredded
1 tablespoon lite (reduced sodium) soy sauce

1. In sprayed non-stick skillet or wok on medium high heat, cook and stir onion and garlic 2 minutes or until onion is tender.

2. Add shredded cabbage, soy sauce and 1 tablespoon water. Cook and stir 4 minutes or until cabbage is crisp-tender.

3. Serve immediately.

Yield: 6 to 8 servings   *Serving size: ¾ cup*

Calories: 29   *Protein: 2 g*   *Carbohydrate: 7 g*
Fat: less than 1 g   *Cholesterol: 0 mg*   *Sodium: 97 mg*
Calcium: 44 mg   *Fiber: 2 g*   *Sugars: 4 g*
Sugar Alcohol: 0 g

Food Exchanges: ½ vegetable

◆

Yellow onions are round or flat in shape, with a mild or sharp flavor. Sweet yellow onions generally have thin, light outer skins, higher water content, and a high sugar content, such as Vidalia onions. They have a fairly short storage life.

⅊ Ratta-Tooey

Net Carbs: 6 g

1 (1 pound) eggplant, peeled, cubed
1 (16 ounce) package frozen seasoning blend (celery, onions,
    peppers, parsley)
1 zucchini, sliced
½ cup Carb Options™ garden-style sauce

1. In Dutch oven over high heat, add eggplant, seasoning
   blend, zucchini and 2 tablespoons water. Heat until
   mixture boils, then reduce heat to low and cover.

2. Cook about 10 to 15 minutes or until vegetables are
   tender. Drain.

3. Return eggplant mixture to Dutch oven. Add ½ cup
   pasta sauce and stir until sauce heats through.

4. If desired, season to taste with salt substitute and
   pepper. Serve hot.

Yield: 6 servings (about 3 cups)   *Serving size: ½ cup*

Calories: 40   *Protein: less than 1 g*   *Carbohydrate: 8 g*
Fat: less than 1 g   *Cholesterol: 0 mg*   *Sodium: 79 mg*
Calcium: 8 mg   *Fiber: 2 g*   *Sugars: 4 g*
Sugar Alcohol: 0 g

Food Exchanges: ½ vegetable

■ ■ ■

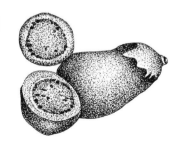

Eggplant-Tomato Casserole

Net Carbs: 7 g

1 (1 to 1¼ pound) eggplant, peeled, cubed
½ cup seasoned breadcrumbs, divided
½ cup Egg Beaters® egg substitute
2 tomatoes, sliced

1. Preheat oven to 350°. In saucepan, heat 2 inches water until it boils. Add eggplant and cook until it is soft.

2. Drain and mash eggplant with fork. Stir in breadcrumbs, egg substitute, salt substitute and pepper to taste.

3. In sprayed 9 x 9-inch baking dish, spread eggplant mixture and top with sliced tomatoes. Sprinkle tomatoes with remaining breadcrumbs and coat with cooking spray.

4. Bake uncovered at 350° for about 25 to 30 minutes or until tomatoes are tender and light brown around edges.

Optional: Over medium heat, cook and stir ⅓ cup chopped onion and 2 minced garlic cloves until onion is clear and tender. Stir into eggplant mixture.

Yield: 8 servings   *Serving size: ½ cup*

Calories: 50   *Protein: 3 g*   *Carbohydrate: 10 g*
Fat: less than 1 g   *Cholesterol: less than 1 g*   *Sodium: 216 mg*
Calcium: 18 mg   *Fiber: 3 g*   *Sugars: 2 g*
Sugar Alcohol: 0 g   *Food Exchanges: ½ bread*

Few of us get enough dietary fiber. The goal should be to eat at least 20 grams of fiber a day.

Oriental Green Beans

Net Carbs: 3 g

1 (16 ounce) package frozen French-style cut green beans
½ cup sliced, rinsed, drained water chestnuts
¼ cup chopped green onion with tops
2 tablespoons lite (reduced sodium) soy sauce

1. Cook green beans according to package directions. Drain.

2. Transfer green beans to medium skillet or saucepan. Add water chestnuts, green onions and soy sauce and mix well. Cook and stir mixture over medium heat until hot. Serve immediately.

Optional: Before serving, sprinkle with chopped salt-free peanuts or toasted, slivered almonds.

Yield: 6 to 8 servings   *Serving size: ½ cup*

Calories: 26   *Protein: 1 g*   *Carbohydrate: 5 g*
Fat: 0 g   *Cholesterol: 0 mg*   *Sodium: 174 mg*
Calcium: 21 mg   *Fiber: 2 g*   *Sugars: 2 g*
Sugar Alcohol: 0 g

Food Exchanges: ½ vegetable

■ ■ ■

Mediterranean Green Beans

Net Carbs: 9 g

1 (16 ounce) package frozen cut green beans
1 onion, chopped
1 to 2 cloves garlic, finely minced
1 (14½ ounce) can diced tomatoes seasoned with Italian herbs or
   other seasoning of choice

1. Cook green beans according to package directions. Drain and set aside.

2. In sprayed skillet or saucepan, cook and stir onions and garlic over medium heat 5 to 6 minutes. Add a few drops water if needed.

3. Pour seasoned tomatoes into onion mixture. Simmer about 10 minutes.

4. Stir in green beans and season to taste with salt substitute and pepper. Simmer until beans heat through.

Yield: 6 to 8 servings   *Serving size: ½ cup*

Calories: 53   *Protein: 2 g*   *Carbohydrate: 11 g*
Fat: less than 1 g   *Cholesterol: 0 mg*   *Sodium: 301 mg*
Calcium: 58 mg   *Fiber: 2 g*   *Sugars: 6 g*
Sugar Alcohol: 0 g

Food Exchanges: 1 vegetable

◆

According to new research, people with diabetes may be healthier if they eat more of their protein from vegetables, beans, and grains, rather than meats.

Citrus-Cumin Black Beans

Net Carbs: 14 g

Black beans never tasted so good!

1 (15 ounce) can black beans, drained, rinsed
½ teaspoon ground cumin or oregano
1 tablespoon frozen orange juice concentrate
1 cup chopped tomatoes or finely chopped red onion

1. In saucepan over low heat, combine beans, cumin and orange juice concentrate and heat through, about 3 to 4 minutes.

2. When ready to serve, garnish each serving with chopped tomatoes and/or red onions.

Tip: Serve with brown or white rice as a main dish.

Yield: 3 to 4 servings   *Serving size: About ½ cup*

Calories: 83	*Protein: 5 g*	*Carbohydrate: 20 g*
Fat: less than 1 g	*Cholesterol: 0 mg*	*Sodium: 251 mg*
Calcium: 46 mg	*Fiber: 6 g*	*Sugars: 2 g*
Sugar Alcohol: 0 g		

Food Exchanges: 2 bread, ½ vegetable

■ ■ ■

Seasoned-Stuffed Mushrooms

Net Carbs: 4 g

12 large mushrooms
1 tablespoon reduced-fat cream cheese (Neufchatel)
2 teaspoons dried herbs
2 tablespoons plain or seasoned breadcrumbs

1. Preheat oven to 350°.

2. Remove stems from mushrooms and chop finely. Place caps on large sprayed baking pan.

3. In sprayed skillet over medium heat, cook and stir chopped mushroom stems 2 to 3 minutes. Stir in cream cheese, herb and breadcrumbs and cook and stir 1 to 2 minutes. Season to taste with salt substitute and pepper.

4. Spoon cream cheese mixture evenly into mushroom caps. Coat with cooking spray. Cover baking pan with aluminum foil and bake about 15 minutes until caps are tender. Remove foil and bake 5 to 6 minutes longer or until tops brown.

Optional: Add 1 tablespoon finely chopped green onions with topsto mushroom stems before cooking in skillet to add more color.

Yield: 4 servings	*Serving size: 3 mushrooms*	
Calories: 37	*Protein: 3 g*	*Carbohydrate: 4 g*
Fat: 2 g	*Cholesterol: 3 mg*	*Sodium: 42 mg*
Calcium: 8 mg	*Fiber: less than 1 g*	*Sugars: 1 g*
Sugar Alcohol: 0 g	*Food Exchanges: 0*	

◆

Non-stick cooking spray and non-stick surface pans should be used to brown or "fry" foods.

Spicy Okra and Tomatoes
Net Carbs: 6 g

1 (16 ounce) package sliced frozen okra, slightly thawed
1 tablespoon canola, peanut or olive oil
1 teaspoon salt-free Creole seasoning
2 (16 ounce) cans no-salt diced tomatoes with liquid

1. In non-stick skillet over medium high heat, cook and stir okra until excess liquid evaporates. When okra starts to stick, add oil. Continue to cook and stir constantly until okra becomes crisp-tender.

2. Stir in seasoning and tomatoes and reduce heat to medium. Cook uncovered, stirring frequently, about 30 minutes.

Variation: *To prepare with fresh okra, heat oil in skillet over medium high heat. Add okra and stir constantly until it is crisp-tender.*

Yield: 8 servings   *Serving size: ½ cup*

Calories: 63   *Protein: 2 g*   *Carbohydrate: 11 g*
Fat: less than 1 g   *Cholesterol: 0 mg*   *Sodium: 76 mg*
Calcium: 81 mg   *Fiber: 5 g*   *Sugars: 4 g*
Sugar Alcohol: 0 g

Food Exchanges: 1 vegetable

◆

Salt substitutes made with potassium chloride have 0 milligrams of sodium.

Skinny Fried Okra

Net Carbs: 6 g

For fans of Southern-fried okra.

2 cups frozen sliced okra
½ teaspoon olive oil
2 to 3 teaspoons cornmeal
½ teaspoon Creole or Cajun seasoning

1. In non-stick skillet over medium heat, cover and cook frozen okra 2 to 3 minutes or until ice melts. Uncover, cook and stir constantly until okra breaks apart.

2. Add oil and cook and stir until okra browns lightly and is tender.

3. Sprinkle with cornmeal and seasoning and stir about 1 minute to mix well.

Yield: 4 servings   *Serving size: ½ cup*

Calories: 46   *Protein: 2 g*   *Carbohydrate: 9 g*
Fat: less than 1 g   *Cholesterol: 0 mg*   *Sodium: 3 mg*
Calcium: 92 mg   *Fiber: 3 g*   *Sugars: 3*
Sugar Alcohol: 0 g

Food Exchanges: 1 vegetable

■ ■ ■

Ranch Pocket Sandwich

Net Carbs: 16 g

4 cups shredded iceberg or romaine lettuce
½ cup chopped roma tomatoes, drained
2 tablespoons Carb Options™ ranch dressing
2 whole-wheat pita breads, cut in half

1. In mixing bowl, lightly toss lettuce, tomatoes and ranch dressing.

2. Open pita bread halves and spoon 1 cup mixture into each.

Optional: Add ½ cup chopped cucumber.

Yield: 4 servings   *Serving size: ½ pocket sandwich*

Calories: 135   *Protein: 4 g*   *Carbohydrate: 20 g*
Fat: 5 g   *Cholesterol: 3 mg*   *Sodium: 225 mg*
Calcium: 25 mg   *Fiber: 4 g*   *Sugars: 1 g*
Sugar Alcohol: 0 g

Food Exchanges: 1 bread, 1 vegetable, 1 fat

■ ■ ■

Twice-Baked Potatoes

Net Carbs: 12 g

4 baking potatoes
1 (8 ounce) package reduced-fat cream cheese (Neufchatel)
1 (8 ounce) carton light sour cream
Choice of garnish: bacon bits, shredded reduced-fat cheddar
    cheese, chopped green onions with tops

1. Preheat oven to 400°.

2. On shallow baking sheet, arrange potatoes. Bake about 45 minutes or until potatoes are tender.

3. Cut potatoes in half lengthwise. Scoop out insides and leave shells intact.

4. In mixing bowl, mix potato with cream cheese and sour cream. Season to taste with salt substitute and pepper.

5. Mound potato filling in potato shells. Sprinkle each potato with choice of garnish.

6. Return potatoes to oven for 5 to 6 minutes and serve hot.

Yield: 8 servings   *Serving size: 1 stuffed potato shell (½ potato)*

Calories (without garnish): 149   *Protein: 6 g*   *Carbohydrate: 12 g*
Fat: 9 g   *Cholesterol: 30 mg*   *Sodium: 133 mg*
Calcium: 82 mg   *Fiber: less than 1 g*   *Sugars: 2 g*
Sugar Alcohol: 0 g   *Food Exchanges: 2 fat, ½ bread*

A plain baked potato has about 160 calories and 0% fat. Adding 2 teaspoons margarine and 2 tablespoons sour cream, however, increases calories to 295 and fat to 46%!

Curried New Potatoes

Net Carbs: 17 g

1 pound small new or red potatoes, scrubbed
1 teaspoon olive oil
¼ to ½ teaspoon curry powder
2 to 3 tablespoons chopped green onions with tops

1. Quarter potatoes and cut in 1-inch wedges. Pat dry with paper towels.

2. In sprayed skillet over medium-high heat, heat oil and add potatoes. Turn potatoes to coat with oil. Cook and stir until potatoes brown and are tender. (Check for tenderness with fork. Skins should be crisp.)

3. In small bowl, combine curry powder and green onions and sprinkle on potatoes. Heat and stir 1 to 2 minutes. Season to taste with black pepper and salt or salt substitute and serve immediately.

Yield: 4 servings (about 2 cups)   *Serving size: ½ cup*

Calories: 94   *Protein: 2 g*   *Carbohydrate: 19 g*
Fat: 1 g   *Cholesterol: 0 mg*   *Sodium: 8 mg*
Calcium: 17 mg   *Fiber: 2 g*   *Sugars: 1 g*
Sugar Alcohol: 0 g

Food Exchanges: 1 bread, ¼ fat

■ ■ ■

❧ Cinnamon-Maple Sweet Potatoes

Net Carbs: 13 g

2 sweet potatoes
2 teaspoons ground cinnamon
1 tablespoon finely grated orange peel
2 tablespoons sugar-free maple syrup

1. Scrub sweet potatoes and prick skins. Cover and cook in microwave on HIGH for 4 minutes on each side or just until potatoes are soft. Let stand 1 to 2 minutes.

2. Scoop potato from shells and mash with fork. Into 3 to 4 small serving bowls, measure ⅓ cup potato. Sprinkle with cinnamon and orange peel and drizzle with syrup.

Yield: 3 to 4 servings   *Serving size: ⅓ cup*

Calories: 66   *Protein: 1 g*   *Carbohydrate: 16 g*
Fat: less than 1 g   *Cholesterol: 0 mg*   *Sodium: 19 mg*
Calcium: 41 mg   *Fiber: 3 g*   *Sugars: 3 g*
Sugar Alcohol: less than 1 g

Food Exchanges: 1 bread, ½ vegetable

■ ■ ■

Sweet Potato Soufflé

Net Carbs: 11 g

2 large sweet potatoes, scrubbed, peeled, quartered
3 to 4 tablespoons Splenda® sugar substitute
2 tablespoons Egg Beaters® egg whites
¼ cup fat-free evaporated milk

1. Preheat oven to 325°. Cut potatoes into pieces, place in saucepan and add water just to cover. Heat until water boils.

2. Reduce heat to simmer, cover and cook 10 to 15 minutes or until potatoes are very tender. Drain. With electric mixer, beat potatoes until smooth.

3. Add remaining ingredients and mix well. In sprayed 1-quart baking dish, spoon potato mixture and bake uncovered 25 minutes.

Yield: 2 cups (4 servings)   *Serving size: ½ cup*

Calories: 66   *Protein: 2 g*   *Carbohydrate: 13 g*
Fat: 0 g   *Cholesterol: 0 mg*   *Sodium: 28 mg*
Calcium: 60 mg   *Fiber: 2 g*   *Sugars: 3 g*
Sugar Alcohol: 0 g

Food Exchanges: 1 bread

■ ■ ■

Crunchy Potato Cakes
Net Carbs: 7 g

1 cup mashed potato flakes
3 tablespoons light sour cream
1 cup crushed bite-size crispy corn cereal squares
2 teaspoons canola, peanut or olive oil

1. Using 1¼ cups water (no milk or margarine), prepare 1 cup mashed potatoes according to package directions.

2. Mix sour cream with potatoes and season to taste with salt substitute and pepper.

3. For 1 potato cake, lightly pack potato mixture into ⅛ cup measuring cup (same size as a coffee measuring cup). Turn out onto palm and roll into 2-inch ball. Flatten into 3-inch cake. Repeat with remaining potato mixture.

4. Preheat non-stick skillet with ½ teaspoon oil over medium high heat. Coat 3 to 4 potato cakes on both sides with crushed cereal and place in hot skillet. Cook about 3 to 4 minutes on each side.

5. With spatula, remove potato cakes from pan and keep warm on baking sheet in 250° oven. Do not cover or cakes will soften.

6. Repeat cooking process with remaining potato cakes. Add only ½ teaspoon oil as needed. Serve immediately.

Yield: About 8 servings   *Serving size: 1 potato cake (1 ounce or ⅛ cup)*
Calories: 46   *Protein: 1 g*   *Carbohydrate: 7 g*
Fat: 2 g   *Cholesterol: 2 mg*   *Sodium: 28 mg*
Calcium: 19 mg   *Fiber: less than 1 g* *Sugars: less than 1 g*
Sugar Alcohol: 0 g
Food Exchanges: ½ bread, ½ fat

Baked Acorn Squash with Apples

Net Carbs: 31 g

1 (1 pound) acorn squash
½ cup Maple Syrup Stir-Fry Apples, (p. 222)

1. Preheat oven to 350°. Cut squash in half lengthwise and remove seeds with spoon.

2. In baking dish with ¼-inch hot water, place squash cut side down. Bake about 1 hour or until squash is tender.

3. Pour water from pan and turn squash right side up. Spoon ¼ cup Stir-Fry Apples into center of each squash and return to oven.

4. Bake 10 minutes or until apples heat through.

Yield: 2 servings   *Serving size: 1 squash half*

Calories: 164   *Protein: 3 g*   *Carbohydrate: 43 g*
Fat: less than 1 g   *Cholesterol: 0 mg*   *Sodium: 1 mg*
Calcium: 104 mg   *Fiber: 12 g*   *Sugars: 16 g*
Sugar Alcohol: 0 g

Food Exchanges: 1 bread, ½ fruit

■ ■ ■

❧ Cheesy Squash Casserole
Net Carbs: 5 g

2 pounds yellow crookneck squash, thinly sliced
¾ cup shredded reduced-fat sharp cheddar cheese, divided
¼ cup light or fat-free mayonnaise
¼ cup Egg Beaters® egg substitute

1. In Dutch oven, cover squash with water and heat until water boils. Cook 8 to 10 minutes or just until squash is tender. Drain well in wire mesh strainer and gently press out liquid with fingers.

2. Preheat oven to 350°.

3. Return squash to Dutch oven, add ½ cup cheese, mayonnaise and egg substitute and mix well. Season to taste with salt substitute and pepper.

4. Spoon into sprayed 1½ to 2-quart baking dish.

5. Sprinkle with remaining ¼ cup cheese.

6. Bake uncovered about 30 minutes.

Yield: 9 servings (about 3 cups)   *Serving size: ½ cup*

Calories: 106   *Protein: 6 g*   *Carbohydrate: 6 g*
Fat: 7 g   *Cholesterol: 16 mg*   *Sodium: 213 mg*
Calcium: 158 mg   *Fiber: 1 g*   *Sugars: 2 g*
Sugar Alcohol: 0 g

Food Exchanges: 1 fat, ½ vegetable

■ ■ ■

Parmesan Rice-Stuffed Squash

Net Carbs: 13 g

2 yellow crookneck squash, washed, trimmed
1 cup cooked brown or white rice
2 tablespoons Egg Beaters® egg substitute
2 tablespoons finely shredded parmesan cheese

1. Cut squash lengthwise and scoop out seeds with spoon.

2. In medium skillet, heat ½ inch water until it boils. Place squash halves cut side down in skillet, cover and simmer 5 minutes. With slotted spoon, turn squash halves cut side up and simmer 5 more minutes or until squash is tender. Remove squash and drain on paper towels.

3. Preheat oven to 350°. In bowl, combine rice and egg substitute and season to taste with black pepper and salt or salt substitute.

4. Mound ¼ cup rice mixture on each squash half. Sprinkle with 2 teaspoons cheese and spray with non-stick cooking spray. Place squash halves on non-stick baking sheet.

5. On non-stick baking sheet, bake squash halves uncovered 15 to 20 minutes or until cheese browns lightly.

Tip: Top each serving with 1 tablespoon heated, low-carb marinara sauce.

Yield: 4 servings	*Serving size: 1 squash half*	
Calories: 87	*Protein: 4 g*	*Carbohydrate: 15 g*
Fat: 1 g	*Cholesterol: 2 mg*	*Sodium: 56 mg*
Calcium: 59 mg	*Fiber: 2 g*	*Sugars: 3 g*
Sugar Alcohol: 0 g	*Food Exchanges: 1 vegetable, ½ starch, ½ lean meat*	

Mediterranean Spinach

Net Carbs: 3 g

½ cup chopped onion
1 (10 ounce) package frozen spinach
¼ cup reduced-fat cottage cheese
¼ cup feta cheese

1. Prepare spinach according to package directions. Drain in wire strainer and squeeze out excess moisture.

2. In sprayed non-stick skillet over medium heat, cook and stir onion until it is tender. Stir in remaining ingredients, cook and stir over low heat until cheeses melt. Season to taste with black pepper.

Tip: Sprinkle each serving with toasted pine nuts or sunflower seeds.

Yield: 3 to 4 servings   *Serving size: ½ cup*

Calories: 72   *Protein: 6 g*   *Carbohydrate: 5 g*
Fat: 3 g   *Cholesterol: 11 mg*   *Sodium: 297 mg*
Calcium: 127 mg   *Fiber: 2 g*   *Sugars: 2 g*
Sugar Alcohol: 0 g

Food Exchanges: 1 vegetable, 1 fat

■ ■ ■

Summer Squash Scramble
Net Carbs: 4 g

⅓ cup chopped green or red bell pepper
⅓ cup chopped onion
1 garlic clove, minced
2 cups cubed yellow crookneck squash

1. Preheat sprayed non-stick skillet over low heat. Add bell pepper, onion and garlic, cook and stir 3 to 4 minutes or until vegetables are tender. Remove from skillet and set aside.

2. Add squash and 2 to 3 tablespoons water to skillet. Bring to simmer over medium heat, then cover and cook 8 to 10 minutes until water evaporates and squash is crisp-tender.

3. Push squash aside and spray skillet with non-stick spray. Return pepper-onion mixture to skillet. Over medium heat, cook and stir until squash heats through and just begins to brown. Season to taste with black pepper and salt or salt substitute.

Yield: 4 to 5 servings   *Serving size: ½ cup*

Calories: 24   *Protein: less than 1 g*   *Carbohydrate: 5 g*
Fat: less than 1 g   *Cholesterol: 0 mg*   *Sodium: 2 mg*
Calcium: 26 mg   *Fiber: 1 g*   *Sugars: 3 g*
Sugar Alcohol: 0 g

Food Exchanges: 1 vegetable

■ ■ ■

Italian-Herbed Tomato Halves

Net Carbs: 12 g

4 tomatoes, halved
3 tablespoons grated parmesan or romano cheese
1 cup Italian-herb-seasoned breadcrumbs

1. Preheat oven to 375°.

2. In shallow baking pan, arrange tomatoes.

3. In mixing bowl, combine cheese and crumbs and season to taste with salt substitute and pepper. Sprinkle crumb mixture over tomato halves.

4. Bake 15 to 20 minutes or until tomatoes heat through and topping browns.

Yield: 8 servings   *Serving size: 1 tomato half*

Calories: 74   *Protein: 3 g*   *Carbohydrate: 13 g*
Fat: 1 g   *Cholesterol: 2 mg*   *Sodium: 429 mg*
Calcium: 42 mg   *Fiber: 1 g*   *Sugars: 2 g*
Sugar Alcohol: 0

Food Exchanges: 1 bread

■ ■ ■

Creamy Mixed Vegetables
Net Carbs: 8 g

1 (16 ounce) frozen vegetable blend (such as broccoli, cauliflower,
  carrot blend)
1 tablespoon margarine or butter (not light)
1 tablespoon all-purpose flour
1¼ cups skim milk

1. Cook vegetables according to package instructions.
   Drain and keep warm.

2. In saucepan over medium heat, melt margarine. Using
   wire whisk, stir in flour and cook about 2 minutes.

3. Add skim milk, cook and stir until sauce thickens.
   Season to taste with salt substitute and pepper.

4. Spoon sauce over vegetables to serve.

*Optional: Add ½ cup reduced-fat shredded Swiss or cheddar
cheese to thickened sauce.*

Yield: 4 to 6 servings   *Serving size: ½ cup*

Calories: 75   *Protein: 3 g*   *Carbohydrate: 10 g*
Fat: 2 g   *Cholesterol: 1 mg*   *Sodium: 76 mg*
Calcium: 79 mg   *Fiber: 2 g*   *Sugars: 5 g*
Sugar Alcohol: 0 mg

Food Exchanges: ½ bread, ½ milk

*Dark green and deep yellow vegetables such as spinach, broccoli,
carrots and sweet potatoes have highest nutritional value.*

Vegetable-Noodle Bowl
Net Carbs: 42 g

1 (16 ounce) package frozen stir-fry vegetables (sugar snap peas,
    onions, mushrooms)
2 cups Swanson® Natural Goodness™ chicken broth
1 cup cooked No Yolk® eggless noodles
2 to 3 tablespoons chopped water chestnuts

1. Cook vegetables until crisp-tender according to package
   directions. Drain and set aside.

2. In medium saucepan, heat chicken broth until it boils.
   Reduce heat, add remaining ingredients and simmer
   until ingredients heat through.

Tip: Serve with reduced-sodium soy sauce.

Yield: About 4 servings   *Serving size: 1 cup*

Calories: 239   *Protein: 10 g*   *Carbohydrate: 46 g*
Fat: 5 g   *Cholesterol: 0 mg*   *Sodium: 329 mg*
Calcium: 13 mg   *Fiber: 4 g*   *Sugars: 5 g*
Sugar Alcohol: 0 g

Food Exchanges: 1 bread, 1 vegetable

■ ■ ■

Roasted Mixed Vegetables
Net Carbs: 3 g

2 pounds or more vegetables (asparagus, bell pepper, broccoli,
   eggplant, mushrooms, squash or onions)
¼ cup canola, peanut or olive oil
2 teaspoons crushed dried herbs (thyme, oregano, tarragon,
   rosemary or herb blend)

1. Preheat oven to 400°.

2. Clean and trim vegetables. In large saucepan, heat
   3 quarts water until it boils. Blanch vegetables
   by adding to boiling water and cooking just until
   vegetables are barely tender.

3. Immediately immerse in cold water and drain on paper
   towels. Continue with remaining vegetables.

4. In roasting pan, lightly toss drained vegetables with oil.
   Roast in oven 5 to 6 minutes or until vegetables brown
   in spots.

5. Season to taste with salt substitute and pepper. Serve
   warm or at room temperature.

Yield: 8 to 10 servings   *Serving size: ½ cup*

Calories: 81   *Protein: 3 g*   *Carbohydrate: 5 g*
Fat: 6 g   *Cholesterol: 0 mg*   *Sodium: 18 g*
Calcium: 35 mg   *Fiber: 2 g*   *Sugars: 2 g*
Sugar Alcohol: 0 g

Food Exchanges: 1 fat, ½ vegetable

■ ■ ■

Ham Fried Rice

Net Carbs: 10 g

1 cup frozen peas and carrots
½ cup cubed turkey ham
1 cup cooked brown rice
¼ cup Egg Beaters® egg substitute

1. In sprayed non-stick skillet over medium heat, cook and stir peas and carrots 2 to 3 minutes or until they thaw. Drain any accumulated water.

2. Reduce heat to low, add ham and rice and heat 3 to 4 minutes until ingredients heat through.

3. Push rice mixture aside and pour egg substitute in skillet. Cook until liquid sets and use a spatula to turn. Do not stir. When egg substitute sets, mix gently with ham-rice mixture.

Tip: Serve with reduced-sodium soy sauce.

Yield: 5 servings (about 2½ cups)   Serving size: ½ cup

Calories: 93   Protein: 7 g   Carbohydrate: 12 g
Fat: 1 g   Cholesterol: 16 mg   Sodium: 298 mg
Calcium: 15 mg   Fiber: 2 g   Sugars: 2 g
Sugar Alcohol: 0 g

Food Exchanges: 1 bread, ½ vegetable, 1 lean meat

■ ■ ■

Fruited Brown Rice

Net Carbs: 14 g

½ cup uncooked brown rice
2 tablespoons raisins
½ cup coarsely chopped orange sections and juice

1. Cook brown rice according to package directions.

2. Stir in raisins and let stand 5 minutes.

3. Just before serving, fold in oranges and juice.

Yield: 4 servings (about 2 cups)   *Serving size: ½ cup*

Calories: 65   *Protein: 1 g*   *Carbohydrate: 15 g*
Fat: less than 1 g   *Cholesterol: 0 mg*   *Sodium: 2 mg*
Calcium: 14 mg   *Fiber: 1 g*   *Sugars: 5 g*
Sugar Alcohol: 0 g

Food Exchanges: 1 bread, 1 fruit

■ ■ ■

Mushroom-Rice Pilaf

Net Carbs: 10 g

1 cup frozen seasoning blend (onions, celery, peppers, parsley)
1 cup coarsely chopped fresh mushrooms
1½ cups Swanson® Natural Goodness™ chicken broth
½ cup uncooked brown rice

1. To sprayed saucepan over medium heat, add frozen seasoning blend. Cook and stir until vegetables are tender. Add water if needed.

2. Add mushrooms, cook and stir about 2 minutes.

3. Gradually add chicken broth and heat until mixture boils. Stir in brown rice, black pepper and salt substitute to taste.

4. Reduce heat, cover and simmer about 50 minutes. Add more broth if needed.

Yield: 8 servings (About 3 cups)   *Serving size: About ⅓ cup*

Calories: 54	*Protein: 2 g*	*Carbohydrate: 10 g*
Fat: less than 1 g	*Cholesterol: 0 mg*	*Sodium: 109 mg*
Calcium: 8 mg	*Fiber: less than 1 g*	*Sugars: less than 1 g*
Sugar Alcohol: 0 g		

Food Exchanges: ½ bread

■ ■ ■

Creamy Spinach with Walnuts
Net Carbs: 3 g

1 (16 ounce) package frozen leaf spinach
1 cup sliced mushrooms
3 tablespoons reduced-fat cream cheese (Neufchatel)
¼ cup chopped walnuts

1. Cook spinach according to package directions. Drain in wire strainer and squeeze out excess moisture.

2. In sprayed non-stick skillet over medium heat, cook and stir mushrooms until they are tender. Drain. Reduce heat to low, add spinach and cream cheese and cook and stir over low heat until cheese melts. Season to taste with black pepper and salt or salt substitute.

3. Top each serving with 2 teaspoons chopped walnuts.

Yield: 4 to 5 servings   *Serving size: ½ cup*

Calories: 104   *Protein: 7 g*   *Carbohydrate: 7 g*
Fat: 7 g   *Cholesterol: 7 mg*   *Sodium: 139 mg*
Calcium: 166 mg   *Fiber: 4 g*   *Sugars: 1 g*
Sugar Alcohol: 0 g

Food Exchanges: 1 vegetable, 1½ fat

■ ■ ■

Creamy Broccoli and Noodles

Net Carbs: 13 g

1 (16 ounce) package frozen broccoli florets or chopped broccoli
1 (3 ounce) package chicken-flavored ramen noodles with flavor
  pack
1 (10¾ ounce) can Campbell's® Healthy Request® cream of
  mushroom condensed soup
½ cup sliced water chestnuts, drained, rinsed

1. In large saucepan or Dutch oven, cook broccoli according to package instructions. Do not overcook. Drain and set aside.

2. In same saucepan, cook noodles according to package instructions and add flavor pack. Stir in broccoli, soup and water chestnuts.

Variation: Substitute 1 cup cooked cubed chicken for water chestnuts.

Yield: 6 to 8 servings (3 to 4 cups)   *Serving size: ½ cup*

Calories: 102   Protein: 3 g   Carbohydrate: 15 g
Fat: 3 g   Cholesterol: 2 mg   Sodium: 368 mg
Calcium: 49 mg   Fiber: 2 g   Sugars: 2 g
Sugar Alcohol: 0 g

Food Exchanges: 1 bread, ½ vegetable, ½ fat

*Stir pasta during the first 1 to 2 minutes
of cooking to keep it from sticking.*

Broccoli-Cheese Mini-Pizza

Net Carbs: 16 g

2 whole-wheat English muffins, split
1½ cups cooked, chopped fresh broccoli or cooked frozen chopped
  broccoli, divided
¾ cup Carb Options™ garden-style sauce
½ cup finely shredded reduced-fat mozzarella or Monterey Jack
  cheese, divided

1. In wire strainer, drain cooked broccoli and spread on
   paper towels.

2. Lightly toast muffin halves. Spread each half with 2 to
   3 tablespoons sauce, ⅓ cup broccoli and 2 tablespoons
   cheese.

Yield: 4 servings   *Serving size: 1 muffin half*

Calories: 144   *Protein: 8 g*   *Carbohydrate: 21 g*
Fat: 4 g   *Cholesterol: 6 mg*   *Sodium: 509 mg*
Calcium: 205 mg   *Fiber: 5 g*   *Sugars: 5 g*
Sugar Alcohol: 0 g

Food Exchanges: 1 vegetable, 1 bread, ½ medium fat meat

■ ■ ■

Green Chili Cheese Casserole
Net Carbs: 8 g

1 (12 ounce) package reduced-carb spaghetti
1 (10 ounce) can mild green chili sauce
1 (10¾ ounce) can Campbell's® Healthy Request® cream of
    mushroom condensed soup
1½ to 2 cups shredded reduced-fat cheddar, jack or mozzarella
    cheese, divided

1. In saucepan, cook spaghetti according to package
   directions.

2. Preheat oven to 350°.

3. Drain spaghetti and return to saucepan. Stir in green
   chili sauce, mushroom soup and 1 cup cheese.

4. Transfer spaghetti mixture to sprayed 9 x 13-inch
   baking dish. Sprinkle remaining ½ cup cheese on top.

5. Bake at 350° for 25 to 30 minutes or until casserole
   bubbles and heats through.

Yield: 16 servings (about 8 cups)   *Serving size: ½ cup*

Calories (without Green Chile Sauce): 154   *Protein: 11 g*
    Carbohydrate: 13 g
Fat: 6 g   *Cholesterol: 16 mg*   *Sodium: 290 mg*
Calcium: 167 mg   *Fiber: 5 g*   *Sugars: less than 1 g*
Sugar Alcohol: 0 mg

Food Exchanges: 1 bread, 1 low fat milk, 1 fat

■ ■ ■

Veggie Tacos
Net carbs: 9 g

1 cup Morningstar Farms® Grillers Burger-Style Veggie Crumbles
4 tablespoons salsa
4 (6 inch) taco shells
4 tablespoons finely shredded reduced-fat Monterey Jack cheese

1. In medium skillet over low heat, stir and heat veggie crumbles, salsa and 3 tablespoons water.

2. On baking sheet in oven, heat taco shells 5 to 6 minutes or until hot and crisp.

3. Spoon ¼ cup mixture into each taco shell and sprinkle with 1 tablespoon cheese.

4. Serve immediately with extra salsa or return tacos to oven to melt cheese.

Tip: Serve with shredded iceberg lettuce and chopped tomatoes.

Yield: 4 servings   *Serving size: 1 taco*

Calories: 135   *Protein: 8 g*   *Carbohydrate: 11 g*
Fat: 7 g   *Cholesterol: 10 mg*   *Sodium: 283 mg*
Calcium: 131 mg   *Fiber: 2 g*   *Sugars: less than 1 g*
Sugar Alcohol: 0 g

Food exchanges: 2½ bread, 1 lean meat, 2 medium fat meat

■ ■ ■

Homemade Mac N Cheese

Net Carbs: 5 g

This is great served with 2 cups reduced-carb elbow, macaroni, penne or rigatoni pasta.

1 tablespoon regular margarine or butter (not light)
1 tablespoon all-purpose flour
1 cup skim milk
4 ounces light processed cheese

1. In heavy saucepan over medium heat, melt margarine. Using wire whisk, stir in flour and cook for 1 minute.

2. Add milk all at once and cook and stir until mixture boils. Boil and stir 1 minute until sauce thickens and is smooth.

3. Remove sauce from heat, add cheese and stir until cheese melts. Season to taste with salt substitute and pepper. Serve with cooked pasta.

Yield: 6 servings   *Serving size: ¼ cup sauce*

Calories (sauce only): 75	*Protein: 5 g*	*Carbohydrate: 5 g*
Fat: 4 g	*Cholesterol: 11 mg*	*Sodium: 340 mg*
Calcium: 38 mg	*Fiber: less than 1 g*	*Sugars: 3 g*
Sugar Alcohol: 0 g	*Food Exchanges: 1 fat, ½ low fat milk, ½ bread*	

◆

Two ounces dry pasta will make about 1 cup cooked pasta. Spaghetti and macaroni products usually double in volume when cooked. Egg noodles don't expand quite as much.

Green Chili Sauce
Net Carbs: 3 g

1 tablespoon margarine or butter (not light)
1½ tablespoons flour
1½ cups Swanson® Natural Goodness™ chicken broth
1 (4 ounce) can mild diced green chilies with liquid

1. In heavy saucepan over medium heat, melt butter and stir in flour. When mixture bubbles, continue to cook and stir 1 minute.

2. Gradually stir in broth and heat until it boils. Cook and stir 1 minute.

3. Add green chilies and simmer 15 to 20 minutes.

4. Use immediately or cover and chill for later use.

Optional: *Add ½ cup finely chopped onion and 1 finely minced garlic clove to butter before adding flour. Add pinch ground cumin.*

Yield: 6 servings (1½ cups) Serving size: ¼ cup

Calories: 31	*Protein: 1 g*	*Carbohydrate: 3 g*
Fat: 2 g	*Cholesterol: 0 mg*	*Sodium: 219 mg*
Calcium: 16 mg	*Fiber: less than 1 g*	*Sugars: less than 1 g*
Sugar Alcohol: 0 g	*Food Exchanges: ½ fat*	

Stock or broth is a strained, thin, clear liquid in which meat, poultry, or fish has been simmered with vegetables and herbs. Make your own or shop for reduced sodium, low fat canned broth.

Tomato-Corn Soup

Net Carbs: 24 g

½ cup chopped onion
3 cups tomato juice
1 cup frozen corn
3 tablespoons reduced-fat sour cream

1. Preheat large sprayed non-stick saucepan over medium heat. Add onions and cook and stir 4 to 5 minutes or until onions are tender.

2. Add tomato juice and corn and simmer 5 minutes. Season to taste with black pepper and salt or salt substitute.

3. To serve, ladle soup into bowls and spoon 1 tablespoon sour cream on each serving.

Variation: Replace corn with 1 cup cooked brown rice.

Yield: 3 servings   *Serving size: 1 cup*

Calories: 128   *Protein: 4 g*   *Carbohydrate: 27 g*
Fat: 2 g   *Cholesterol: 6 mg*   *Sodium: 665 mg*
Calcium: 53 mg   *Fiber: 3 g*   *Sugars: 13 g*
Sugar Alcohol: 0 g

Food Exchanges: 1 vegetable, ½ bread, ⅓ fat

■ ■ ■

Tex-Mex Black Bean Soup
Net Carbs: 12 g

⅓ cup finely chopped onion
½ clove garlic, minced or pressed
¼ teaspoon dried oregano leaves or ground cumin
1 (15½ ounce) can black beans with liquid

1. Preheat sprayed large saucepan over medium heat. Add chopped onion and garlic and cook and stir 2 to 3 minutes. Stir in oregano and cook about 1 minute longer. Remove from heat.

2. In food processor or blender, process beans with liquid until desired consistency (chunky or smooth). For thinner soup, add small amount water.

3. Pour bean puree in saucepan with onion and garlic mixture. Heat until mixture boils, reduce heat and simmer 10 minutes for flavors to blend. Season to taste with salt substitute and pepper.

Yield: 4 servings   *Serving size: ½ cup*

Calories: 106   *Protein: 7 g*   *Carbohydrate: 20 g*
Fat: less than 1 g   *Cholesterol: 0 mg*   *Sodium: 422 mg*
Calcium: 44 mg   *Fiber: 8 g*   *Sugars: less than 1 g*
Sugar Alcohol: 0 g

Food Exchanges: 1½ bread

◆

Mince – cut into tiny, irregular pieces about ⅛ inch in size.

Spicy Southwestern Soup
Net Carbs: 1 g

4 (14 ounce) cans Swanson® Natural Goodness™ chicken broth
1 (10 ounce) can mild diced tomatoes and green chilies with liquid
1 to 2 teaspoons chili powder
½ teaspoon ground cumin

1. In large saucepan or Dutch oven, combine all ingredients.

2. Simmer 30 minutes for flavors to blend.

Optional: Serve with No-Guilt Tortilla Crisps, (p. 30).

Yield: 8 servings   *Serving size: 1 cup*

Calories: 10 g   *Protein: 1 g*   *Carbohydrate: 1 g*
Fat: less than 1 g   *Cholesterol: 0 mg*   *Sodium: 204 mg*
Calcium: 20 mg   *Fiber: less than 1 g* *Sugars: less than 1 g*
Sugar Alcohol: 0 g

Food Exchanges: 0

■ ■ ■

Emergency Chicken-Noodle Soup

Net Carbs: 9 g

1 (3 ounce) package chicken-flavored ramen noodles and flavor
  pack
2 (14 ounce) cans Swanson® Natural Goodness™ chicken broth
1 cup frozen peas and carrots or mixed vegetables
1 cup cubed cooked chicken breasts

1. Prepare noodles according to package directions and set aside.

2. In large saucepan, heat chicken broth until it boils. Add vegetables and cook 4 to 5 minutes. Add chicken and noodles and season to taste with salt substitute and black pepper.

Yield: 8 servings   *Serving size: 1 cup*

Calories: 94   *Protein: 8 g*   *Carbohydrate: 9 g*
Fat: 3 g   *Cholesterol: 15 mg*   *Sodium: 438 mg*
Calcium: 7 mg   *Fiber: less than 1 g*   *Sugars: 1 g*
Sugar Alcohol: 0 g

Food Exchanges: ½ bread, ½ fat

■ ■ ■

Vegetable Soup with Herbs
Net Carbs: 8 g

3 (14 ounce) cans Swanson® Natural Goodness™ chicken broth
Soup Herb Blend (below) or other salt-free seasoning blend to
   taste
1 (16 ounce) package frozen vegetables for soup mix (tomatoes,
   potatoes, corn, carrots, butter beans, okra, green beans,
   onions, celery)

1. In large pot, pour broth and heat until it boils.

2. Stir in Soup Herb Blend and frozen vegetables. Reduce
   heat and simmer 15 to 20 minutes.

3. Remove bay leaf and serve hot.

Optional: Add ⅛ teaspoon garlic powder with herbs.

Yield: 6 servings (6 cups)   *Serving size: 1 cup*

Calories: 45   *Protein: 3 g*   *Carbohydrate: 8 g*
Fat: 0 g   *Cholesterol: 0 mg*   *Sodium: 508 mg*
Calcium: 0 mg   *Fiber: less than 1 g*   *Sugars: 3 g*
Sugar Alcohol: 0 g

Food Exchanges: ½ vegetable

■ ■ ■

Main Dishes
Beef

No-Beans Chili
Net Carbs: 5 g

1 onion, finely chopped
1 (1 pound) package lean ground beef
1 (10 ounce) can mild diced tomatoes and green chilies
1 (1.25 ounce) packet reduced-sodium taco seasoning mix

1. In sprayed large skillet over medium heat, cook and stir onion until tender. Do not brown. Remove and set aside.

2. In same skillet over medium heat, cook and stir ground beef until it browns. Transfer to wire mesh strainer and drain. Wipe skillet with paper towels to remove excess fat.

3. Return meat and onion to skillet. Stir in tomatoes, taco seasoning and 1 to 2 cups water. Simmer 25 to 30 minutes for flavors to blend.

Optional: Serve with No-Guilt Tortilla Crisps, (p. 30).

Yield: 8 servings   *Serving size: ½ cup*

Calories: 131   *Protein: 13 g*   *Carbohydrate: 5 g*
Fat: 6 g   *Cholesterol: 36 g*   *Sodium: 366 mg*
Calcium: 23 mg   *Fiber: less than 1 g* *Sugars: 3 g*
Sugar Alcohol: 0 g

Food Exchanges: 1½ medium fat meat, ½ other carb, ½ vegetable

Chop – cut into small, irregular pieces about ¼ inch in size.

⅔ Oven-Barbecued Brisket

Net Carbs: 1 g

3 pounds lean brisket, trimmed
1½ to 2 tablespoons Mrs. Dash® salt-free blend or
   Steak Grilling Blend™
1 cup Carb Options™ barbecue sauce

1. Preheat oven to 275°.

2. On large piece heavy duty, wide aluminum foil, place brisket and sprinkle generously on both sides with seasoning blend.

3. Seal brisket tightly in foil. Bake 2½ hours (or 1 hour per pound) and remove from oven to check for tenderness. When brisket is fork-tender, drain meat juices and reserve. Brush 1 cup barbecue sauce on brisket. Continue cooking for 20 to 30 minutes.

4. Remove brisket from oven. Transfer to baking pan or dish, seal tightly and chill. Pour reserved meat juices in separate container and chill. After juices cool, remove any congealed fat.

5. To prepare for serving, slice cold brisket across grain of meat. Lay slices in 9 x 13-inch or smaller baking dish. Pour reserved liquid over brisket.

6. Heat at 300° until meat heats through.

Tip: Be sure to trim all visible fat from brisket.

Yield: 20 servings   Serving size: 1 slice (3 ounces) brisket

Calories: 149	Protein: 22 g	Carbohydrate: 1 g
Fat: 5 g	Cholesterol: 27 mg	Sodium: 167 mg
Calcium: 13 mg	Fiber: 0 g	Sugars: 0 g
Sugar Alcohol: 0 g	Food Exchanges: 3 lean meat	

Quick and Easy
Beef-Stuffed Peppers
Net Carbs: 6 g

3 large green bell peppers, whole
1 onion, finely chopped
1 (1 pound) package lean ground beef
2 cups Carb Options™ garden-style sauce

1. Cut peppers lengthwise into 2 halves. Remove stems, seeds and white membrane.

2. In medium saucepan, heat about 4 cups water until it boils. Drop peppers into boiling water and boil 5 to 6 minutes or until peppers are crisp tender. Plunge into cold water and set upside down on paper towels to drain.

3. Preheat oven to 350°.

4. In sprayed nonstick skillet over medium heat, cook and stir onion until tender. Remove from skillet and set aside.

5. Add ground beef to skillet, cook and stir until it browns. Drain meat in wire mesh strainer and wipe skillet with paper towels to remove any accumulated fat.

6. In skillet, combine ground beef, onion and 1 cup sauce. Mound mixture into peppers. Bake covered 20 minutes. Remove cover.

7. While peppers bake, heat remaining sauce in small saucepan. Spoon sauce over baked peppers and serve immediately.

Yield: 6 servings	*Serving size: 1 stuffed pepper half with sauce*	
Calories: 247	*Protein: 16 g*	*Carbohydrate: 9 g*
Fat: 16 g	*Cholesterol: 52 mg*	*Sodium: 412 mg*
Calcium: 16 mg	*Fiber: 3 g*	*Sugars: 5 g*
Sugar Alcohol: 0 g	*Food Exchanges: 2 fat, ½ medium fat meat, ½ vegetable*	

Spaghetti Meat Sauce

Net Carbs: 4 g

½ (1 pound) package lean ground beef
½ (1 pound) package ground turkey
1 (1 pound 10 ounce) jar Carb Options™ garden-style sauce
1 to 2 teaspoons dried basil or oregano

1. In sprayed large skillet over medium heat, cook meat until it browns. Drain in wire mesh strainer. Wipe skillet with paper towels to remove any accumulated fat.

2. Return meat to skillet and add sauce, herbs and 1 cup water and mix well. Cover and simmer 30 minutes to allow flavors to blend.

Optional: Try Mrs. Dash® Salt-Free Classic Italian Seasoning Blend instead of basil or oregano for a little different flavor.

Yield: 8 servings   *Serving size: ½ cup*

Calories: 166   *Protein: 12 g*   *Carbohydrate: 5 g*
Fat: 10 g   *Cholesterol: 42 mg*   *Sodium: 437 mg*
Calcium: 7 mg   *Fiber: 1 g*   *Sugars: 3 g*
Sugar Alcohol: 0 g

Food Exchanges: 1½ medium fat meat, ½ vegetable

"Hamburger" meat may have added seasonings, fillers or fat—so choose clearly labeled "lean ground beef."

❧ Spicy Beef Enchiladas

Net Carbs: 11 g

¾ (1 pound) package lean ground beef or turkey breast
2 (10 ounce) cans mild red chili enchilada sauce, divided
8 (8 inch) low-carb tortillas
1½ cups reduced-fat shredded cheddar, jack or mozzarella cheese

1. Preheat oven to 375°. In skillet over medium heat, cook and stir ground beef until it browns. Drain meat in wire mesh strainer to remove fat. Wipe skillet with paper towels to remove any accumulated fat. Reduce heat to low, return meat to skillet and mix with 1 can enchilada sauce. Cook and stir over low heat until sauce mixes well.

2. Spoon about 2 tablespoons meat mixture near edge of each tortilla. Add 1 to 2 tablespoons cheese, then roll tortilla and place seam side down in sprayed 11 x 7-inch or 9 x 9-inch baking dish. (If tortillas do not roll easily, heat between damp paper towels 10 to 15 seconds on HIGH power in microwave.)

3. Coat rolled tortillas with cooking spray. Bake 15 minutes.

4. While enchiladas are baking, heat half remaining can enchilada sauce in saucepan. Store remaining sauce for later use.

5. Remove enchiladas from oven and spread with hot enchilada sauce. Top with remaining cheese. Return to oven 5 to 10 minutes or until cheese melts. Serve immediately.

Yield: 8 enchiladas
Calories (with sauce): 369
Fat: 20 g
Calcium: 337 mg
Sugar Alcohol: 0 g
Serving size: 1 enchilada
Protein: 25 g
Cholesterol: 58 mg
Fiber: 13 g
Carbohydrate: 24 g
Sodium: 694 mg
Sugars: 5 g
Food Exchanges: 2½ medium fat meat, 1 bread, 1 fat, ½ vegetable

Stir-Fry Steak and Bok Choy

Net Carbs: 1 g

½ pound lean boneless flank or top sirloin steak, trimmed
1 head bok choy
3 teaspoons canola, peanut or olive oil
1 cup Stir-Fry Cooking Sauce (p. 214)

1. Slice steak into 1 x 3-inch thin strips and set aside.

2. Wash bok choy carefully and cut leaves from stems. Cut stems in ¼-inch slices and shred leaves.

3. Heat non-stick surface wok or large skillet over high heat. Add 1 teaspoon oil and bok choy stems. Cook uncovered, stirring constantly, 1 to 2 minutes.

4. Add ¼ cup water, cover and cook additional 2 minutes. Add leaves and cook and stir 1 to 2 more minutes. Remove bok choy from wok.

5. Pour remaining 2 teaspoons oil into wok. When oil is hot, add steak. Cook and stir until meat browns slightly, about 3 to 4 minutes.

6. Stir in Stir-Fry Cooking Sauce and return bok choy to wok. Cook and stir until sauce boils and thickens.

Yield: 4 servings   *Serving size: 1 cup*

Calories (without sauce): 137   *Protein: 14 g*   *Carbohydrate: 2 g*
Fat: 8 g   *Cholesterol: 24 mg*   *Sodium: 65 mg*
Calcium: 101 mg   *Fiber: 1 g*   *Sugars: less than 1 g*
Sugar Alcohol: 0 g

Food Exchanges: 1 fat, ½ medium fat meat

■ ■ ■

Mama's Meat Loaf
Net Carbs: 9 g

1 (14½ ounces) can stewed tomatoes with Mexican flavors
  (jalapeno, garlic and cumin), divided
1 (1 pound) package lean ground beef or turkey breast
½ cup Egg Beaters® egg substitute
1 cup old-fashion rolled oats, uncooked

1. Preheat oven to 350°.

2. In food processor or blender, process tomatoes about 5 to 10 seconds. In mixing bowl, combine all ingredients and season to taste with salt substitute and pepper.

3. Pack meat mixture in sprayed 9 x 5 x 3-inch loaf pan.

4. Bake about 1½ hours or until meat cooks. Drain fat from loaf pan 1 to 2 times during cooking.

Yield: About 6 servings   *Serving size: 1 (1 inch) slice*

Calories: 215   *Protein: 17 g*   *Carbohydrate: 9 g*
Fat: 12 g   *Cholesterol: 51 mg*   *Sodium: 410 mg*
Calcium: 53 mg   *Fiber: less than 1 g*   *Sugars: 4 g*
Sugar Alcohol: 0 g

Food Exchanges: 2 medium fat meat, 1 bread, ½ fat, ½ vegetable

Beef-Stuffed Cabbage Rolls
Net Carbs: 5 g

1 (2½ pound) large head cabbage
1 (16 ounce) package frozen seasoning blend (onions, celery,
   peppers, parsley), slightly thawed
1 (1 pound) package lean ground beef or ground turkey breast
¼ cup Egg Beaters® egg substitute

1. Remove 10 to 12 large leaves from cabbage. Trim thick
   rib from back of each leaf to be even with rest of leaf.
   Immerse leaves in boiling water 5 to 6 minutes or until
   thick part is crisp-tender. Remove and drain.

2. In sprayed skillet over medium heat, cook and stir
   seasoning blend until liquid evaporates and vegetables
   are tender. Remove from skillet and set aside.

3. Add ground beef to skillet and cook and stir until meat
   browns. Drain meat in wire mesh strainer.

4. Wipe skillet with paper towels and return seasoning
   blend and meat to skillet. Season to taste with salt
   substitute and pepper. Stir in egg substitute.

5. Place 1 to 2 tablespoons meat mixture near end of each
   cabbage leaf. Roll leaves to enclose meat mixture and
   tuck ends under.

6. In steamer basket in large pot or electric steamer,
   arrange 1 layer cabbage rolls. Steam each batch 15 to
   20 minutes or until cabbage is tender.

Yield: 10 to 12 servings
Calories: 122
Fat: 5 g
Calcium: 53 mg
Sugar Alcohol: 0 g

Serving size: 1 cabbage roll
Protein: 11 g   *Carbohydrate: 8 g*
Cholesterol: 29 mg   *Sodium: 67 mg*
Fiber: 3 g   *Sugars: 5 g*
Food Exchanges: ½ medium fat meat, ½
vegetable, ½ fat

Wild Rice-Stuffed Cabbage Rolls

Net Carbs: 19 g

8 large cabbage leaves
1 (6 ounce) package reduced-sodium long grain and wild rice mix
1 cup reduced-fat shredded Swiss or jack cheese, divided
1 (4 ounce) can no-salt tomato sauce

1. Cook rice according to package directions. While rice is cooking, prepare cabbage leaves.

2. Trim rib from the back of each cabbage leaf to be even with the rest of the leaf. In saucepan, heat water until it boils. Immerse cabbage leaves in boiling water 5 to 6 minutes or until leaves wilt. Drain.

3. In mixing bowl, combine ¾ cup cheese and 1½ cups cooked rice (reserve remaining rice for later use).

4. Spoon 2 to 3 tablespoons rice mixture onto cabbage leaf. Roll sides of leaf over rice mixture, then fold in both ends of leaf.

5. In steamer basket in large pot or electric steamer, place rolls seam side down and steam 30 to 35 minutes or until cabbage is tender.

6. Heat tomato sauce and season to taste with salt substitute and pepper. Pour over cooked cabbage rolls and sprinkle with remaining ¼ cup cheese. Let stand until cheese melts.

Variation: Instead of steaming cabbage rolls, pour tomato sauce over rolls and bake at 350° for 35 to 40 minutes or until cabbage is tender. Remove from oven and sprinkle cheese on top.

Yield: 8 servings
Calories: 221
Fat: 9 g
Calcium: 368 mg
Sugar Alcohol: 0 g

Serving size: 1 cabbage roll with sauce
Protein: 13 g
Cholesterol: 25 mg
Fiber: 1 g
Food Exchanges: 1 bread, 1 medium fat meat, ½ vegetable, ½ fat

Carbohydrate: 20 g
Sodium: 346 mg
Sugars: 2 g

Main Dishes
Pork

⋇ Grilled Pork Chops with Apples
Net Carbs: 0 g

4 (3 x 4 inch) boneless pork chops
½ teaspoon Mrs. Dash® Chicken Grilling Blend™
Maple Syrup Stir-Fry Apples (p. 222)

1. Sprinkle pork chops with seasoning. Using outdoor grill, grill pork chops covered at 350° to 400° for about 10 minutes on each side. (To cook indoors, broil uncovered in oven about 10 minutes on each side.) Top pork chops with Maple Syrup Stir-Fry Apples.

Yield: 4 servings   *Serving size: 1 boneless pork chop*

Calories (without apples): 169   *Protein: 25 g*   *Carbohydrate: 0 g*
Fat: 7 g   *Cholesterol: 62 mg*   *Sodium: 41 mg*
Calcium: 5 mg   *Fiber: 0 g*   *Sugars: 0 g*
Sugar Alcohol: 0 g

Food Exchanges: 3½ lean meat

■ ■ ■

No-Fuss Pork Chop Packets
Net Carbs: 7 g

4 small boneless pork chops, trimmed
1 teaspoon garlic powder
1 white or yellow onion, sliced
1 red or green apple, unpeeled, cored, cut in thick wedges

1. Preheat oven to 325°. On each of 4 large (18 inch) pieces aluminum foil, place 1 pork chop. Sprinkle with ¼ teaspoon garlic powder, salt substitute and pepper to taste. Add sliced onions and apple wedges. Seal pork chops tightly. Bake for 1 hour or until pork chops are tender.

Tip: Be sure to use garlic powder, not garlic salt.

Yield: 4 servings   *Serving size: 1 pork chop pouch*

Calories: 240   *Protein: 23 g*   *Carbohydrate: 8 g*
Fat: 13 g   *Cholesterol: 66 mg*   *Sodium: 51 mg*
Calcium: 31 mg   *Fiber: 1 g*   *Sugars: 5 g*
Sugar Alcohol: 0 g

Food Exchanges: 3 medium fat meat, 1 fruit, ½ vegetable

■ ■ ■

Fancy Grilled Ham and Cheese
Net Carbs: 13 g

2 slices low-carb whole wheat bread
2 to 3 teaspoons brown or dijon-style mustard
2 slices 98% fat-free deli ham
1 slice fat free swiss cheese

1. Preheat skillet over medium heat.

2. Spread mustard on one slice bread and add ham and cheese.

3. Spray one side of sandwich with cooking spray and cook that side in skillet until it browns.

4. Spray other side with cooking spray and cook until it browns.

5. Serve warm.

Optional: Serve with 1 large dill pickle.

Yield: 1 serving   *Serving size: 1 sandwich*

Calories: 155   *Protein: 22 g*   *Carbohydrate: 17 g*
Fat: 3 g   *Cholesterol: 12 mg*   *Sodium: 825 mg*
Calcium: 6 mg   *Fiber: 4 g*   *Sugars: 3 g*
Sugar Alcohol: 0 g

Food Exchanges: 3 very lean meat, 1 bread

■ ■ ■

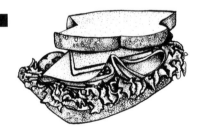

Hot Dog Wraps
Net Carbs: 14 g

4 (8 to 10 inch) low-carb or whole wheat tortillas
4 regular size fat-free frankfurters
4 mozzarella string cheese sticks, pulled apart
Your choice of condiments (pickle relish, mustard, sugar-free
  ketchup)

1. Preheat oven to 375°.

2. Spray one side of tortillas with cooking spray and place
   a hot dog about 1 inch from edge of each.

3. Split hot dog down middle and insert cheese. Add
   condiments. Roll up hot dog inside tortilla.

4. In sprayed baking dish, place tortilla wraps seam side
   down. Coat each wrap with cooking spray.

5. Bake 10 to 15 minutes or until hot dog heats and
   cheese melts. If tortillas begin to dry out, remove from
   oven and spray with cooking spray, then return to oven.

Yield: 4 servings   *Serving size: 1 hot dog wrap*

Calories: 231   *Protein: 18 g*   *Carbohydrate: 25 g*
Fat: 7 g   *Cholesterol: 28 mg*   *Sodium: 993 mg*
Calcium: 219 mg   *Fiber: 11 g*   *Sugars: 2 g*
Sugar Alcohol: 0 g

Food Exchanges: 1½ bread, 1 fat, ½ lean meat

■ ■ ■

Skillet Pork Medallions with Apples and Onions

Net Carbs: 4 g

Medallion – a small, round piece of meat usually beef, veal or pork.

1 (¾ to 1 pound) pork tenderloin
1 onion
1 cooking apple (Granny Smith, Fuji or Gala)
½ cup Swanson® Natural GoodnessTM chicken broth, divided

1. Cut tenderloin in ¾-inch crosswise slices (meat cuts more easily if slightly frozen). Season to taste with salt or salt substitute and black pepper.

2. Peel onion, cut in half and cut each half into slices. Peel and core apple and cut into thin slices.

3. In sprayed non-stick skillet over medium-high heat, brown medallions. Remove from skillet and set aside. Add sliced onions and apples to skillet. Stir and cook until onions brown and become tender.

4. Return pork medallions to skillet. Add ⅓ cup chicken broth. Bring to boil and reduce heat to simmer. Cook about 5 minutes and add remaining chicken broth if needed. Remove pork, onions and apples and keep warm in serving dish. Over medium-high heat, reduce liquid until it thickens slightly. Season to taste with salt or salt substitute and pepper. Pour over pork dish and serve.

Yield: 6 to 8 servings *Serving size: 1 pork medallion with apples and onions*

Calories: 139 *Protein: 18 g* *Carbohydrate: 4 g*
Fat: 5 g *Cholesterol: 52 mg* *Sodium: 71 mg*
Calcium: 12 mg *Fiber: less than 1 g* *Sugars: 3 g*
Sugar Alcohols: 0 g *Food Exchanges: 3 lean meat*

Main Dishes
Chicken & Turkey

Chicken-Cream Cheese Rolls

Net Carbs: less than 1 g

4 small boneless, skinless chicken breasts
4 tablespoons reduced-fat cream cheese
2 tablespoons chopped green onions with tops
4 slices turkey bacon

1. Preheat oven to 350°. To thin chicken breasts, place in resealable plastic bag and pound with rolling pin until chicken breast is ¼-inch thick. Season to taste with black pepper.

2. Combine cream cheese and green onions and place equal amount on each chicken breast. Roll chicken breast around cream cheese mixture. Wrap 1 slice bacon around each chicken roll and secure roll with wooden pick or cotton string.

3. In sprayed baking dish, bake rolls uncovered 30 minutes. Chicken is done when juices run clear and meat is no longer pink. Remove picks or string before serving.

Tip: Reduced-fat cream cheese is also called Neufchatel.

Yield: *4 servings*   Serving size: *1 roll*

Calories: *164*	Protein: *23 g*	Carbohydrate: *less than 1 g*
Fat: *8 g*	Cholesterol: *69 mg*	Sodium: *488 mg*
Calcium: *12 mg*	Fiber: *0 g*	Sugars: *less than 1 g*
Sugar Alcohol: *0 g*		

Food Exchanges: *3 very lean meat, 1 fat*

■ ■ ■

Lemon-Garlic Baked Chicken

Net Carbs: less than 1 g

1 tablespoon fresh lemon juice
1 tablespoon canola, peanut or olive oil
1 clove garlic, finely minced
1 (2½ to 3 pound) whole chicken, cut into serving pieces

1. Preheat oven to 350°. In small bowl, combine lemon juice, oil, garlic and salt substitute and pepper to taste.

2. In shallow baking dish, arrange chicken in single layer. Pour lemon juice mixture over chicken.

3. Cover and bake, basting occasionally, about 45 minutes or until chicken is tender and juices run clear.

Yield: 6 to 8 servings   *Serving size: 1 to 2 pieces chicken*

Calories: 134   *Protein: 13 g*   *Carbohydrate: less than 1 g*
Fat: 9 g   *Cholesterol: 46 mg*   *Sodium: 135 mg*
Calcium: 4 mg   *Fiber: less than 1 g*   *Sugars: less than 1 g*
Sugar Alcohol: 0 g

Food Exchanges: 1 medium fat meat, ½ fat

■ ■ ■

Curried Chicken

Net Carbs: 5 g

1 (10¾ ounce) can Campbell's® Healthy Request® cream of
  mushroom condensed soup
1 teaspoon curry powder
4 boneless, skinless chicken breast halves, cooked, cubed
⅓ cup slivered almonds, toasted

1. In large saucepan, combine soup, ½ soup can water and
   curry. Stir in cubed chicken. Heat and stir until mixture
   heats through. Sprinkle with almonds just before
   serving.

Yield: 6 servings   *Serving size: ⅔ cup*

Calories: 185   *Protein: 25 g*   *Carbohydrate: 6 g*
Fat: 7 g   *Cholesterol: 59 mg*   *Sodium: 455 mg*
Calcium: 59 mg   *Fiber: 1 g*   *Sugars: 1 g*
Sugar Alcohol: 0 g

Food Exchanges: 1 lean meat, ½ other carb, ½ fat

■ ■ ■

"Fried" Chicken

Net Carbs: 16 g

1 cup skim milk
4 boneless, skinless chicken breast halves
1 to 1½ cups whole grain or whole wheat Melba toast crumbs
1 teaspoon dried herbs or Mrs. Dash® salt-free seasoning blend of
   your choice

1. In container with lid, soak chicken breasts in milk.
   Cover and chill about 30 minutes.

2. Preheat oven to 375°.

3. Mix toast crumbs and seasoning. Drain chicken breasts
   and coat with crumbs, pressing crumbs lightly on both
   sides of chicken with fingers.

4. On lightly sprayed baking sheet, place chicken. Bake
   20 minutes and check for doneness by piercing chicken
   with knife. Chicken is done when meat is tender and
   juices run clear.

Yield: 4 servings   *Serving size: 1 chicken breast*

Calories: 261   *Protein: 38 g*   *Carbohydrate: 17 g*
Fat: 4 g   *Cholesterol: 86 mg*   *Sodium: 594 mg*
Calcium: 64 mg   *Fiber: 1 g*   *Sugars: 3 g*
Sugar Alcohol: 0 g

Food Exchanges: 4½ very lean meat, 1 bread, ½ milk

■ ■ ■

Citrus-Baked Chicken

Net Carbs: less than 1 g

1 lime
⅓ cup lite (reduced sodium) soy sauce
½ teaspoon ground ginger
4 small boneless, skinless chicken breast halves

1. Finely grate ½ teaspoon lime peel and squeeze 1 tablespoon lime juice.

2. In small saucepan, combine soy sauce, lime peel and juice, ginger and 3 tablespoons water. Heat mixture until it boils and boil 1 minute. Cool to room temperature.

3. In resealable plastic bag or container, place chicken breasts and pour cooled marinade over chicken. Refrigerate several hours or overnight.

4. Preheat oven to 350°.

5. Pour off marinade. In sprayed baking dish, bake chicken covered about 45 minutes or until chicken is tender and juices run clear.

6. Uncover and brown chicken breasts under oven broiler 5 minutes on each side.

Yield: 4 servings *Serving size: 1 chicken breast half*
Calories: 190 *Protein: 35 g* *Carbohydrate: less than 1 g*
Fat: 4 g *Cholesterol: 96 mg* *Sodium: 228 mg*
Calcium: 20 mg *Fiber: less than 1 g* *Sugars: less than 1 g*
Sugar Alcohol: 0 g *Food Exchanges: 5 very lean meat*

♦

Four ounces raw meat is equal to 3 ounces cooked meat, or 3 meat exchanges. Weigh meat portions after cooking and removing bones and fat.

❧ Ultimate Broccoli-Cheese Chicken

Net Carbs: 5 g

¼ cup pine nuts or slivered almonds
2 (10 ounce) packages frozen broccoli florets in cheese sauce
3 cups cubed cooked chicken or turkey breasts
¼ cup diced pimentos

1. In dry skillet over medium heat, cook and stir nuts until they brown.

2. Cook frozen broccoli in sauce according to package directions.

3. Transfer to large saucepan and stir in chicken and pimentos.

4. Simmer, stirring constantly, until chicken and broccoli mixture heats through. Add water if necessary to thin sauce. Season to taste with salt substitute and pepper. Remove from heat and keep warm.

5. Sprinkle mixture with toasted nuts just before serving.

Yield: 6 to 8 servings   *Serving size: ⅔ cup*

Calories: 244   *Protein: 34 g*   *Carbohydrate: 7 g*
Fat: 9 g   *Cholesterol: 84 mg*   *Sodium: 448 mg*
Calcium: 59 mg   *Fiber: 2 g*   *Sugars: 4 g*
Sugar Alcohol: 0 g

Food Exchanges: 1½ lean meat, ½ vegetable, ½ fat

■ ■ ■

Chicken-Mushroom Oven Packets

Net Carbs: 5 g

1 cup sliced fresh mushrooms, divided
1 sliced yellow or white onion, divided
4 small boneless, skinless chicken breast halves
8 tablespoons Carb Options™ olive oil vinaigrette dressing

1. Preheat oven to 350°.

2. On each of 4 (18 inch) pieces aluminum foil, place mushrooms, onions and then chicken breasts. Season chicken with salt substitute and pepper.

3. Fold up sides of foil and spoon 2 tablespoons dressing into each packet.

4. Seal packet tightly and bake 30 minutes. Open packet and baste chicken and vegetables with dressing. Reseal packet and continue baking for additional 30 minutes.

5. Serve in packet or remove to serving plate.

Yield: 4 servings   *Serving size: 1 chicken breast and vegetables*

Calories: 253   *Protein: 37 g*   *Carbohydrate: 5 g*
Fat: 11 g   *Cholesterol: 85 mg*   *Sodium: 644 mg*
Calcium: 9 mg   *Fiber: less than 1 g*   *Sugars: 3 g*
Sugar Alcohol: 0 g

Food Exchanges: 5 lean meat, ½ vegetable

■ ■ ■

Teriyaki Chicken Tenders
Net Carbs: 9 g

1 pound boneless, skinless chicken tenders
⅓ cup plus 2 teaspoons Carb Options™ Asian teriyaki marinade,
  divided
¼ cup sliced green onions with tops
1 (8 ounce) can pineapple chunks or tidbits, juice reserved

1. In resealable plastic bag, place tenders and marinade. Refrigerate and marinate 15 to 20 minutes.

2. Preheat sprayed non-stick wok or skillet over high heat. Add about ½ chicken tenders and stir-fry 2 minutes or until chicken browns. Remove first batch cooked chicken and keep warm. Repeat with remaining chicken.

3. Add green onions, pineapple with 1 tablespoon pineapple juice and 1 to 2 teaspoons marinade to wok and cook and stir about 1 minute.

4. Spoon onions and pineapple over chicken tenders and serve immediately.

Variation: Substitute 1 pound cubed lean boneless pork for chicken tenders.

Yield: 4 servings   *Serving size: 2 chicken tenders*

Calories: 141   *Protein: 22*   *Carbohydrate: 9 g*
Fat: 6 g   *Cholesterol: 66 mg* *Sodium: 688 mg*
Calcium: 5 mg   *Fiber: less than 1 g* *Sugars: 7 g*
Sugar Alcohol: 0 mg

Food Exchanges: 3 lean meat, ½ fruit

■ ■ ■

Cheesy Chicken Spaghetti
Net Carbs: 12 g

1 (12 ounce) package low-carb spaghetti
1 (16 ounce) package light processed cheese, cubed, divided
½ cup diced tomatoes and green chilies, drained, reserve liquid
2 cups cubed cooked chicken

1. In saucepan, prepare spaghetti according to package directions. Drain and return to saucepan.

2. Preheat oven to 350°.

3. Set aside ¼ cup cheese. In microwave-safe dish, mix remaining cheese and tomatoes and green chilies and cover. Heat mixture on HIGH for 1½ minutes. Remove, stir and return to microwave for additional 1½ minutes. Stir and let stand.

4. Combine cheese mixture with cooked spaghetti and chicken. If needed, add 1 tablespoon reserved tomato liquid.

5. Transfer to 9 x 13-inch baking dish and top with reserved cheese.

6. Bake, covered, about 25 to 30 minutes or until mixture bubbles and heats through.

Yield: 12 to 14 servings   *Serving size: ½ cup*

Calories: 202   *Protein: 20 g*   *Carbohydrate: 18 g*
Fat: 4 g   *Cholesterol: 37 mg*   *Sodium: 660 mg*
Calcium: 4 mg   *Fiber: 6 g*   *Sugars: 3 g*
Sugar Alcohol: 0 g

Food Exchanges: 2 lean meat, 1 bread, 1 other carb

■ ■ ■

❧ Chicken and Dumplings

Net Carbs: 4 g

¼ cup plus 3 tablespoons reduced-fat baking mix
¼ teaspoon crushed dried thyme
2 (14 ounce) cans Swanson® Natural Goodness™ chicken broth
1 (12½ ounce) can 98% fat-free premium chicken breast in water or
   2 cups cooked cubed chicken breasts

1. Stir baking mix and 3 tablespoons water to make soft dough. Add small amount baking mix if dough is too sticky. Add thyme, salt substitute and pepper to taste.

2. In medium saucepan over high heat, combine broth and chicken and heat until mixture boils. Drop dumpling mixture by tablespoonfuls onto boiling broth.

3. Reduce heat to medium (slow boil, not a simmer) and cook uncovered 10 minutes. Cover and continue cooking 10 more minutes.

4. Ladle into small bowls to serve.

Tip: Use the reduced-fat baking mix for biscuits, pancakes, dumplings.

Yield: About 6 servings (6 small dumplings plus chicken and broth)
Serving size: ½ to ¾ cup (1 dumpling plus chicken and broth)

Calories: 77	*Protein: 11 g*	*Carbohydrate: 4 g*
Fat: 1 g	*Cholesterol: 21 mg*	*Sodium: 554 mg*
Calcium: 0 g	*Fiber: 0 g*	*Sugars: less than 1 g*
Sugar Alcohol: 0 g		

Food Exchanges: 1½ very lean meat

■ ■ ■

Chicken Italiano
Net Carb: 7 g

4 boneless, skinless chicken breast halves, rinsed, patted dry
¼ cup fat-free or light mayonnaise
¼ cup Italian seasoned breadcrumbs
¼ cup grated parmesan or romano cheese

1. Preheat oven to 375°. Lightly spread mayonnaise on both sides of each chicken breast. In flat dish, mix breadcrumbs and cheese. Add salt substitute and pepper to taste.

2. Coat chicken with crumb mixture and transfer to baking sheet. (Cover baking sheet with aluminum foil for easier cleaning.) Bake 45 minutes or until chicken is tender and juices run clear.

Yield: 4 servings   *Serving size: 1 chicken breast half*

Calories: 269   *Protein: 37 g*   *Carbohydrate: 7 g*
Fat: 10 g   *Cholesterol: 94 mg*   *Sodium: 684 mg*
Calcium: 65 mg   *Fiber: less than 1 g*   *Sugars: 1 g*
Sugar Alcohol: 0 g

Food Exchanges: 1½ lean meat, 1 fat, ½ bread

■ ■ ■

Rosemary-Garlic Chicken

Net Carbs: less than 1 g

4 small boneless, skinless chicken breasts
1 clove garlic, finely minced
2 to 3 teaspoons dried rosemary, crushed
¼ to ½ cup Swanson® Natural Goodness™ chicken broth

1. With paper towels, pat chicken dry and season to taste with salt or salt substitute and black pepper.

2. In sprayed non-stick skillet over medium-high heat, brown chicken on both sides. Remove from heat and add garlic and rosemary.

3. Return skillet to medium heat and cook and stir chicken about 1 minute. Be careful not to burn garlic.

4. Add ¼ cup chicken broth to skillet and simmer gently 30 minutes. Add chicken broth as needed.

5. Pierce chicken with sharp knife to test for doneness. Juices should run clear and chicken should not be pink. Pour remaining broth over chicken to serve.

Tip: Replace rosemary with tarragon for a different flavor.

Yield: 4 servings   *Serving size: 1 chicken breast (3 to 4 ounces)*

Calories: 103   *Protein: 20 g*   *Carbohydrate: less than 1 g*
Fat: 2 g   *Cholesterol: 49 mg*   *Sodium: 273 mg*
Calcium: 11 mg   *Fiber: less than 1 g* *Sugars: 0 g*
Sugar Alcohol: 0 g

Food Exchanges: 3 very lean meat

■ ■ ■

Chicken and Wild Rice Supreme

Net Carbs: 21 g

1 (6 ounce) package reduced-sodium long grain and wild rice mix
2 boneless, skinless chicken breasts, cooked, cubed
1 (10¾ ounce) can Campbell's® Healthy Request® cream of
    mushroom condensed soup
1 (4 ounce) jar diced pimentos with liquid

1. Prepare rice according to package directions. Preheat
   oven to 350°. Mix all ingredients and ¼ cup water. Pour
   into sprayed 11 x 7-inch or 9 x 9-inch baking dish.
   Cover and bake 25 minutes or until mixture bubbles
   and heats through.

Yield: About 8 cups   *Serving size: 1 cup*

Calories: 183   *Protein: 14 g*   *Carbohydrate: 22 g*
Fat: 4 g   *Cholesterol: 31 mg*   *Sodium: 424 mg*
Calcium: 41 mg   *Fiber: 1 g*   *Sugars: 1 g*
Sugar Alcohol: 0 g

Food Exchanges: 1½ lean meat, 1 bread, ½ other carb

■ ■ ■

*One small chicken thigh, ½ cup tuna or ½ cup
cottage cheese are equivalent to 2 ounces meat.*

Outdoor Fizzy Chicken
Net Carbs: 7 g

1 (2 to 3 pound) whole fryer, trimmed
2 tablespoons Mrs. Dash® Chicken Grilling Blend, divided
1 (12 ounce) can reduced-carb cola or diet cola
1½ cups Carb Options™ barbecue sauce

1. Rub inside cavity of chicken with 1½ teaspoons seasoning. Coat outside of chicken with non-stick cooking spray.

2. Pour out ½ can cola and make 2 to 3 additional holes in can top. Spoon remaining seasoning into cola can. With chicken held upright, place chicken cavity on cola can, pulling legs out to form a tripod.

3. Light 1 side of grill and preheat to medium.

4. Set chicken upright on grill away from direct heat source. Cover with grill lid and cook about 1 hour or until chicken turns golden and registers 180° when meat thermometer is inserted in leg or breast.

5. Let stand 5 minutes and serve with barbecue sauce.

Tip: Be sure to trim all fat and skin from chicken for the most nutritious dish.

Yield: 4 to 6 servings	*Serving size: ½ chicken breast or 1 leg plus 2 tablespoons barbecue sauce*	
Calories: 183	*Protein: 24 g*	*Carbohydrate: 7 g*
Fat: 6 g	*Cholesterol: 74 mg*	*Sodium: 418 mg*
Calcium: 11 mg	*Fiber: 0 g*	*Sugars: 4 g*
Sugar Alcohol: 0 g	*Food Exchanges: 3½ lean meat, ½ other carb*	

■ ■ ■

Chicken with Sugar Snap Peas
Net Carbs: 4 g

1(16 ounce) package frozen sugar snap peas
1 (8 ounce) package mushrooms, cleaned, sliced
2 boneless, skinless chicken breasts, cooked, cut into thin strips
⅓ cup Sweet and Sour Sauce (p. 210)

1. Cook sugar snap peas according to package instructions. Immediately rinse in cool water to stop cooking, drain and set aside.

2. In sprayed large skillet over medium heat, cook and stir mushrooms 5 to 6 minutes or until mushrooms are tender.

3. Add peas, chicken strips and Sweet and Sour Sauce and stir until mixture heats through. Season to taste with salt substitute and pepper.

4. Serve immediately.

Optional: Sprinkle with 1 tablespoon toasted sesame seeds.

Yield: 8 servings
Calories (without sauce): 71
Fat: 1 g
Calcium: 42 mg
Sugar Alcohol: 0 g
Food Exchanges: 1½ lean meat, ½ vegetable

Serving size: 1 cup
Protein: 11 g
Cholesterol: 21 mg
Fiber: 2 g

Carbohydrate: 6 g
Sodium: 110 mg
Sugars: 3 g

◆

To make green pepper strips or slices, hold the pepper upright on a cutting surface. Slice each of the sides from the pepper stem and discard stem, white membrane and seeds. You should have 4 large, flat pieces of pepper that are easy to slice or chop.

Low-Carb Chicken Fajitas
Net Carbs: 14 g

1 cup sliced yellow or white onion
1 cup green or red bell peppers, cut in strips
1 oven-broiled or charcoal-grilled boneless, skinless chicken
    breast, cut in strips
4 low-carb whole wheat tortillas

1. Preheat oven to 300°.

2. In sprayed large skillet, cook and stir onions and bell peppers over medium heat until they are slightly brown and tender. Add chicken breast strips and heat. Season to taste with salt substitute and pepper.

3. Seal tortillas in aluminum foil and warm in oven about 5 minutes. To use microwave oven, place damp towels between tortillas and heat on high power only 5 to 6 seconds.

4. Transfer ingredients to serving platter and serve immediately.

Optional: Add 1 garlic clove, minced, to onion and peppers. Provide toppings such as light or fat free sour cream, salsa and/or Wakka-Moley (p. 31).

Yield: 4 servings   *Serving size: 1 fajita*
Calories: 178   *Protein: 17 g*   *Carbohydrate: 15 g*
Fat: 5 g   *Cholesterol: 21 mg*   *Sodium: 664 mg*
Calcium: 12 mg   *Fiber: 1 g*   *Sugars: 3 g*
Sugar Alcohol: 0 g
Food Exchanges: 2 lean meat, 1 bread, ½ vegetable

◆

Thaw frozen foods in refrigerator or in the microwave, never at room temperature, which allows unsafe bacterial growth.

Chicken-Cheese Quesadillas
Net Carbs: 5 g

2 large boneless, skinless chicken breasts, cut into strips
1½ cups seasoning blend (onion, peppers, celery, parsley)
8 (8 inch) low-carb whole wheat tortillas
1 cup shredded reduced-fat cheddar cheese

1. In sprayed non-stick skillet over medium heat, cook chicken strips until meat is no longer pink. During cooking, add seasoning blend and cook and stir until onions are tender. Reduce heat to low.

2. Transfer chicken to cutting board and dice. Return chicken to skillet and mix with seasoning blend. Season to taste with salt substitute and pepper.

3. On each of 4 tortillas, spoon ¼ chicken mixture. Top with cheese and cover with another tortilla.

4. Spray skillet again with cooking spray. In batches, cook each quesadilla on both sides until tortillas brown, spraying liberally with cooking spray as needed. Keep cooked quesadillas warm.

5. Cut each quesadilla into 4 wedges and serve with light sour cream and salsa.

Yield: 8 servings (16 quesadilla wedges)   *Serving size: 2 wedges*

Calories: 210   *Protein: 20 g*   *Carbohydrate: 8 g*
Fat: 12 g   *Cholesterol: 42 mg*   *Sodium: 561 mg*
Calcium: 202 mg   *Fiber: 3 g*   *Sugars: less than 1 g*
Sugar Alcohol: 0 g

Food Exchanges: 1 fat, 1 medium fat meat, ½ bread

■ ■ ■

⅛ Chicken-Cream Cheese Burrito

Net Carbs: 8 g

1 (8 inch) low-carb whole wheat tortilla
1 tablespoon reduced-fat cream cheese (Neufchatel)
1 to 2 tablespoons chopped cooked chicken breast
2 teaspoons chopped green onions with tops

1. Preheat oven to 400°.

2. Spread cream cheese near edge of tortilla. Add chicken and green onion. Roll tortilla and place seam side down on sprayed baking sheet.

3. Spray tortilla with cooking spray and heat 5 to 6 minutes or until cream cheese melts and tortilla browns slightly.

Optional: Serve with 1 tablespoon salsa.

Yield: 1 burrito

Calories: 160   *Protein: 9 g*   *Carbohydrate: 19 g*
Fat: 5 g   *Cholesterol: 16 mg*   *Sodium: 382 mg*
Calcium: 21 mg   *Fiber: 11 g*   *Sugars: less than 1 g*
Sugar Alcohol: 0 g

Food Exchanges: 1 medium fat meat, 1 bread

■ ■ ■

Black Bean Quesadillas
Net Carbs: 6 g

1 cup canned black beans, drained, rinsed
1 cup mild or medium salsa, divided
12 (8 inch) low-carb whole wheat tortillas
1 cup reduced-fat cheddar, jack or mozzarella cheese

1. In mixing bowl, mash beans with fork and combine with ¼ cup salsa.

2. Spray tortillas on both sides with non-stick cooking spray. Spoon bean mixture on 6 tortillas, spreading almost to edges. Sprinkle with cheese and top with remaining tortillas.

3. Preheat sprayed griddle or skillet over medium heat until hot. Place 1 quesadilla on griddle and cook 2 to 3 minutes or until it begins to brown. Turn and cook 1 to 2 minutes.

4. Repeat with remaining quesadillas. Cut each into 6 wedges and serve hot with remaining salsa.

Optional: Add ¼ cup chopped green onion with tops and 3 tablespoons finely chopped cilantro to bean mixture.

Variation: Substitute pinto beans for black beans.

Yield: 12 servings   *Serving size: 3 to 4 wedges*
Calories: 133 g   *Protein: 11 g*   *Carbohydrate: 15 g*
Fat: 7 g   *Cholesterol: 14 mg*   *Sodium: 361 mg*
Calcium: 202 mg   *Fiber: 9 g*   *Sugars: less than 1 g*
Sugar Alcohol: 0 g
Food Exchanges: 1 medium fat meat, 1 bread, ½ vegetable

■ ■ ■

Crunchy Turkey Slaw
Net Carbs: 7 g

1 cup diced and cooked turkey or chicken breasts
1 (10 ounce) package angel-hair cabbage slaw or 5 cups finely
    shredded green cabbage
1 cup sliced celery
3 tablespoons Soy Sauce Dressing (p. 216) or oil and vinegar

1. In large bowl, lightly toss turkey or chicken, cabbage and celery.

2. Cover and chill before serving.

3. Just before serving, drizzle with Soy Sauce Dressing and toss lightly. Serve immediately.

Optional: *Sprinkle salad with 1 tablespoon toasted sesame seeds, toasted slivered almonds or toasted crushed ramen noodles before serving.*

Variation: *Substitute ½ cup sliced, rinsed water chestnuts for celery.*

Yield: 6 servings
Calories (without dressing): 52
Fat: less than 1 g
Calcium: 37 mg
Sugar Alcohol: 0 g

Serving size: 1 cup
Protein: 4 g
Cholesterol: 5 g
Fiber: 2 g
Food Exchanges: ½ lean meat, ½ vegetable

Carbohydrate: 9 g
Sodium: 85 mg
Sugars: 2 g

■ ■ ■

Turkey Pita Lunch
Net Carbs: 20 g

2 whole-wheat pita breads
8 thin slices deli turkey
2 cups fresh vegetables (alfalfa spouts, cucumber and tomato
  slices)
2 tablespoons sunflower seeds

1. Cut pita breads in half. Fill each half with 2 slices turkey and ½ cup fresh vegetables. Garnish with ½ tablespoon sunflower seeds.

Tip: Spread 1 tablespoon mustard on each pita half.

Yield: 4 servings   *Serving size: ½ pita bread*

Calories: 149   *Protein: 9 g*   *Carbohydrate: 23 g*
Fat: 4 g   *Cholesterol: 13 mg*   *Sodium: 430 mg*
Calcium: 14 mg   *Fiber: 3 g*   *Sugars: 3 g*
Sugar Alcohol: 0 g

Food Exchanges: 1 bread, 1 very lean meat, ½ vegetable

■ ■ ■

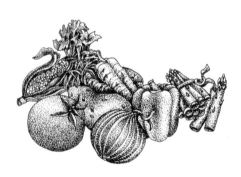

Turkey Burgers
Net Carbs: 4

½ cup finely chopped onion
2 slices low-carb wheat bread
1 (1 pound) package ground turkey breast
1 cup grated zucchini

1. In sprayed skillet over medium heat, cook and stir onions until tender, adding few drops water if needed. Remove from skillet and set aside.

2. In food processor or blender, process bread until crumbs are fine. (Breadcrumbs should measure 1 cup).

3. In mixing bowl, lightly mix onion, breadcrumbs, turkey and zucchini. Season to taste with salt substitute and pepper.

4. Form mixture into 5 to 6 patties. In sprayed skillet over medium heat, place patties and cook 3 to 4 minutes on each side. Do not overcook or meat will be dry.

Yield: 5 to 6 patties   *Serving size: 1 patty*

Calories: 207   *Protein: 24 g*   *Carbohydrate: 6 g*
Fat: 10 g   *Cholesterol: 74 mg*   *Sodium: 147 mg*
Calcium: 31 mg   *Fiber: 2 g*   *Sugars: 2 g*
Sugar Alcohol: 0 g

Food Exchanges: 3 lean meat, ½ bread

Vegetarian products such as soy burgers contain processed soybean protein, also known as textured vegetable protein.

Chunky Sloppy Joes

Net Carbs: 4 g

½ pound (1 cup lightly packed) ground white turkey breast
1 cup frozen pepper stir-fry (sliced green, red, yellow bell peppers
    and white onions)
¼ cup no-salt tomato sauce
4 to 5 tablespoons Carb Options™ barbecue sauce

1. In sprayed non-stick skillet over medium heat, brown and crumble turkey. Remove from skillet and set aside.

2. In same skillet, cook and stir peppers and onions until they brown lightly.

3. Return cooked turkey to skillet and add tomato sauce, barbecue sauce and 3 to 4 tablespoons water. Simmer about 8 minutes and add water if needed. Season to taste with salt or salt substitute and black pepper.

Tip: Serve on sugar-free whole wheat hamburger buns.

Yield: 4 servings (2 cups)   Serving size: ½ cup

Calories (without bun): 81 Protein: 13 g   Carbohydrate: 4 g
Fat: less than 1 g   Cholesterol: 23 mg   Sodium: 243 mg
Calcium: 7 mg   Fiber: less than 1 g   Sugars: 2 g
Sugar Alcohol: 0 g

Food Exchanges: 2 very lean meat, 1 vegetable

■ ■ ■

Pepperoni-Pita Pizza

Net Carbs: 14 g

2 (6 inch) whole-wheat pita breads, split
24 slices turkey pepperoni
¾ cup Carb Options™ garden-style sauce or marinara sauce
½ cup finely shredded reduced-fat mozzarella or Monterey Jack
cheese

1. Lightly toast split pita bread. Spread 2 to 3 tablespoons sauce, 6 slices pepperoni and 2 tablespoons cheese on each pita half.

2. Broil 2 to 3 minutes or until cheese melts. Serve immediately.

Yield: 4 servings   *Serving size: 1 pita half*

Calories: 150   *Protein: 10 g*   *Carbohydrate: 17 g*
Fat: 5 g   *Cholesterol: 20 mg*   *Sodium: 641 mg*
Calcium: 124 mg   *Fiber: 3 g*   *Sugars: 3 g*
Sugar Alcohol: 0 g

Food Exchanges: ½ vegetable, 1 bread, 1 lean meat

■ ■ ■

Bite-size—cut into pieces about 1 inch in size.

Spaghetti and Meatballs

Net Carbs: 11 g

1 (12 ounce) package frozen Italian-style turkey meatballs
1 (12 ounce) package reduced-carb spaghetti
1 (8 ounce) package fresh mushrooms, sliced
3 cups Homemade Spaghetti Sauce (p. 209) or 3 cups Carb
　Options™ garden-style sauce

1. Heat meatballs according to package directions for baking in conventional or microwave oven.

2. While meatballs are heating, prepare spaghetti according to package directions.

3. In sprayed skillet over medium heat, cook and stir mushrooms 5 minutes or until tender.

4. Combine mushrooms, meatballs and pasta sauce. Serve 1 meatball and ¼ cup sauce with ½ cup cooked spaghetti.

Yield: 12 servings　　*Serving size: 1 meatball with pasta and sauce*

Calories (without sauce): 162　*Protein: 14 g*　*Carbohydrate: 18 g*
Fat: 3 g　*Cholesterol: 22 mg*　*Sodium: 314 mg*
Calcium: less than 1 mg　*Fiber: 7 g*　*Sugars: 1 g*
Sugar Alcohol: 0 g

Food Exchanges: 1 bread, ½ lean meat

■ ■ ■

⋧ Delicious Low-Carb Lasagna

Net Carbs: 4 g

4 to 6 zucchini squash, cut in lengthwise slices
1 (1 pound) ground turkey breast
2 cups Carb Options™ garden-style sauce
1 cup shredded reduced-fat mozzarella or jack cheese

1. Preheat oven to 350°.

2. In large skillet or Dutch oven, heat ½ cup water until it boils. Reduce heat. Add zucchini, reduce heat, cover and simmer until zucchini is clear and tender. Drain and set aside.

3. Spray dry skillet with cooking spray and add ground turkey. Cook and stir until turkey turns white.

4. Add pasta sauce and ¼ cup water. Simmer 15 to 20 minutes to blend flavors.

5. In sprayed 9 x 13-inch baking dish, place zucchini in single layer. Pour meat sauce over zucchini. Cover and bake 15 to 20 minutes or until mixture bubbles and heats through.

6. Uncover and sprinkle with cheese. Return to oven 5 minutes or until cheese melts.

Variation: Substitute 1 (1 pound) package lean ground beef for turkey. Drain fat from meat and skillet before adding pasta sauce.

Yield: About 10 servings   Serving size: ¾ to 1 cup
Calories: 117   Protein: 15 g   Carbohydrate: 6 g
Fat: 4 g   Cholesterol: 23 mg   Sodium: 315 mg
Calcium: 90 mg   Fiber: 2 g   Sugars: 3 g
Sugar Alcohol: 0 g
Food Exchanges: 2 lean meat, 1 other carb, ½ vegetable

Turkey or Chicken Teriyaki Packet

Net Carbs: 4 g

2 (5 x 4 x ¼ inch) turkey steaks or 2 boneless, skinless chicken
   breast halves
1 cup sliced fresh mushrooms, divided
½ red bell pepper, slivered, divided
2 tablespoons Carb Options™ Asian teriyaki marinade

1. Preheat oven to 350°.

2. On each of 2 large pieces aluminum foil, place turkey steaks and season to taste with pepper.

3. Top each with ½ cup sliced mushrooms and ¼ cup red pepper. Spoon on 1 tablespoon marinade.

4. Fold aluminum foil to make tight seal around turkey and vegetables.

5. Bake 15 minutes. Remove from oven and spoon sauce on mushrooms and peppers. Reseal and bake another 10 to 15 minutes or until vegetables are tender and turkey is white and tender.

6. Serve in opened packets or transfer turkey, vegetables and sauce to dinner plate.

Yield: 2 servings   *Serving size: 1 packet*

Calories: 221   *Protein: 35 g*   *Carbohydrate: 5 g*
Fat: 12 g   *Cholesterol: 86 mg*   *Sodium: 582 mg*
Calcium: 32 mg   *Fiber: 1 g*   *Sugars: 3 g*
Sugar Alcohol: 0 g

Food Exchanges: 5 lean meat

Turkey Meatballs Carbonara
Net Carbs: 4 g

1 (12 ounce) package frozen Italian-style turkey meatballs
1 yellow or white onion, thinly sliced
4 slices turkey bacon, cut into pieces
1 (1 pound) jar Carb Options™ alfredo sauce

1. Follow package directions for heating meatballs in conventional or microwave oven.

2. In sprayed large skillet, cook and stir onion and bacon until onion is tender and bacon cooks. (Spray skillet again if needed.)

3. Mix ⅓ cup water and alfredo sauce. Add to skillet with onion and bacon. Bring to boil and reduce heat to simmer. Add cooked meatballs and heat through.

Optional: Serve each meatball with ¼ cup sauce over ⅓ cup cooked reduced-carb pasta.

Yield: 12 meatballs   *Serving size: 1 meatball with sauce*

Calories: 139   *Protein: 6 g*   *Carbohydrate: 5 g*
Fat: 10 g   *Cholesterol: 44 mg*   *Sodium: 529 mg*
Calcium: 2 mg   *Fiber: 1 g*   *Sugars: less than 1 g*
Sugar Alcohol: 0 g

Food Exchanges: 1 fat, ½ bread, ½ high fat meat, ½ vegetable

The sharpness of white onions and red onions can be reduced by storing in the refrigerator.

✹ Roasted Cornish Hens with Fresh Orange Relish

Net Carbs: 14 g

2 (1¼ to 1½ pound) frozen cornish hens
2 oranges
¼ cup dried cranberries or raisins
1 tablespoon chopped pecans

1. Thaw hens according to package instructions. Preheat oven to 450°. Rinse hens and pat dry inside and outside with paper towels.

2. Spray roasting pan and hens with non-stick cooking spray. Season hens with salt substitute and pepper to taste. Place roasting pan on middle rack in oven.

3. Roast hens uncovered about 50 minutes until juices run clear when a wood pick or fork is inserted in meaty part of the hen or when an inserted meat thermometer registers 180°.

4. While hens roast, prepare orange relish. Grate 2 teaspoons orange peel, remove peel, separate into sections and cut in ½-inch pieces.

5. In small bowl, combine orange pieces, dried cranberries and pecans. Transfer to serving dish and sprinkle orange peel on top. Cover and chill until serving time.

6. When ready to serve, cut hens in half lengthwise. Serve with fresh orange relish.

Yield: 4 servings
Calories: 407
Fat: 3 g
Calcium: 53 mg
Sugar Alcohol: 0 g

Serving size: ½ hen and ¼ cup relish
Protein: 30 g   *Carbohydrate: 16 g*
Cholesterol: 168 mg   *Sodium: 84 mg*
Fiber: 2 g   *Sugars: 11 g*
Food Exchanges: 3 fat, 1 medium fat meat, 1 fruit

Main Dishes
Seafood

Shrimp-Avocado Feast
Net Carbs: 2 g

1 head romaine or leaf lettuce
2 ripe avocados
1 pound cooked, peeled, veined shrimp
4 tablespoons Lemon Oil Dressing (p. 215)

1. With knife, cut out large lettuce ribs or stems. Roll lettuce and hold while cutting in ¼-inch pieces. Pile lettuce on 4 salad plates.

2. Halve each avocado and remove seed. With peel still on, cut each half into 4 wedges. With fingers, carefully pull peel away. Arrange wedges on lettuce.

3. Arrange shrimp on top of avocado. Drizzle each plate with 1 tablespoon dressing and serve immediately.

Yield: 4 servings   *Serving size: 1½ cups*

Calories (without dressing): 212   *Protein: 17g*   *Carbohydrate: 9g*
Fat: 13 g   *Cholesterol: 0 mg*   *Sodium: 551 mg*
Calcium: 84 mg   *Fiber: 7 g*   *Sugars: 2 g*
Sugar Alcohol: 0 g

Food Exchanges: 1½ fat, ½ medium fat meat, ½ vegetable

■ ■ ■

Shrimp Alfredo
Net Carbs: 2 g

1 cup frozen cooked, peeled, veined shrimp
½ cup Carb Options™ alfredo sauce
1 tablespoon chopped roasted red pepper

1. In skillet over medium heat, stir frozen shrimp until it thaws. Drain in wire strainer.

2. Reduce heat to low, add sauce and red pepper and heat through. Add shrimp just before serving.

Tip: *Serve over ⅓ cup cooked whole-wheat fettuccine or cholesterol-free noodles.*

Yield: 3 servings   *Serving size: About 1 cup*

Calories: 154   *Protein: 16*   *Carbohydrate: 2 g*
Fat: 8 g   *Cholesterol: 135 mg*   *Sodium: 372 mg*
Calcium: 40 mg   *Fiber: 0 g*   *Sugars: less than 1 g*
Sugar Alcohol: 0 g

Food Exchanges: 1 very lean meat, 2 fat

❧ Shrimp Florentine

Net Carbs: 3 g

2 (10 ounce) bags fresh spinach, rinsed
2 to 3 teaspoons corn starch
2 pounds frozen cooked, peeled, veined shrimp
Lemon-pepper seasoning to taste

1. In sprayed large skillet, cook spinach 3 to 5 minutes over medium heat or until it is limp.

2. Mix corn starch with 2 to 3 teaspoons water and stir until it dissolves. Add corn starch mixture to skillet, bring to boil and stir until it thickens.

3. Add shrimp and seasoning. Reduce heat to low and cook until shrimp heats through.

4. Serve immediately.

Yield: 8 servings   *Serving size: About 1 generous cup*

Calories: 140   *Protein: 25 g*   *Carbohydrate: 4 g*
Fat: 2 g   *Cholesterol: 172 mg*   *Sodium: 313 mg*
Calcium: 130 mg   *Dietary Fiber: 1 g*   *Sugars: 0 g*
Sugar Alcohol: 0 g

Food Exchanges: 3½ very lean meat

■ ■ ■

Speedy Shrimp Creole
Net Carbs: 7 g

1 (16 ounce) package frozen seasoning blend (onions, celery, peppers, parsley)
1 cup sliced fresh mushrooms
1 (14½ ounce) can diced tomatoes
1 pound fresh shrimp, peeled, veined

1. In large skillet over medium heat, cook and stir seasoning blend, mushrooms and ¼ cup water until vegetables are tender and liquid evaporates. Add tomatoes with liquid and simmer 15 to 20 minutes.

2. Add shrimp and cook about 10 minutes more or until shrimp turn pink and are tender. Season to taste with salt substitute and pepper.

3. Serve immediately.

Tip: You may substitute 1 (16 ounce) package frozen peeled, veined shrimp.

Optional: Add few dashes hot pepper sauce.

Yield: *About 6 to 8 servings* Serving size: *½ cup*
Calories: *110*   Protein: *14 g*   Carbohydrate: *8 g*
Fat: *1 g*   Cholesterol: *98 mg*   Sodium: *246 mg*
Calcium: *53 mg*   Fiber: *1 g*   Sugars: *5 g*
Sugar Alcohol: *0 g*   Food Exchanges: *2 very lean meat, ½ vegetable*

■ ■ ■

❧ Crawfish Spaghetti Sauce
Net Carbs: 5 g

Serve this sauce over cooked reduced-carb spaghetti.

1 (10 ounce) can diced tomatoes and green chiles
1 (1 pound) package frozen cleaned, peeled crawfish tails
1 (10 ounce) can Campbell's® Healthy Request® cream of chicken
  condensed soup
½ (15 ounce) jar light processed cheese spread

1. In skillet over medium heat, heat tomatoes.

2. Add crawfish and cook and stir 10 minutes.

3. Add soup and cheese and mix well. Season with salt substitute and pepper to taste.

4. Serve over cooked pasta.

Tip: You may substitute diced tomatoes with Italian herbs for a different flavor. They are both good.

Yield: 12 servings   Serving size: About ½ cup

Calories (without pasta): 85   Protein: 74 g   Carbohydrate: 5 g
Fat: 3 g   Cholesterol: 65 mg   Sodium: 492 mg
Calcium: 9 mg   Fiber: less than 1 g Sugars: 2 g
Sugar Alcohol: 0 g

Food Exchanges: 3 very lean meat, ½ vegetable

◆

To test doneness of cooked pasta, lift a piece and quickly bite into it. It should be tender, but still firm or al dente (to the tooth).

Salmon Patties
Net Carbs: 9 g

1 (12 ounce) can salmon
⅓ cup finely chopped onion
¼ cup Egg Beaters® egg substitute
11 multigrain or reduced-fat saltine crackers, crushed

1. Drain and clean salmon of excess skin. Flake with fork. Stir in onion, egg substitute and about ¼ cup cracker crumbs.

2. Pack salmon mixture for each patty into ⅓ measuring cup. Flatten slightly and coat with crushed crackers.

3. Preheat non-stick skillet over high heat. Liberally spray 1 side of each patty with cooking spray. Place patty-sprayed side down in skillet. Reduce heat to medium.

4. Cook each patty for 3 minutes, spray top side of patty and turn carefully with spatula. Cook 2 to 3 more minutes or until patty turns golden brown.

5. Transfer each patty to serving plate and keep warm until all patties cook.

Yield: 6 servings (6 patties) Serving size: 1 patty

Calories: 129	*Protein: 12 g*	*Carbohydrate: 9 g*
Fat: 4 g	*Cholesterol: 20 mg*	*Sodium: 434 mg*
Calcium: 11 mg	*Fiber: less than 1 g*	*Sugars: 2 g*
Sugar Alcohol: 0 g		

Food Exchanges: ½ bread, ½ lean meat, ½ fat

■ ■ ■

Low-Fat Tuna Melt

Net Carbs: 13 g

1 (6 ounce) can solid white albacore tuna in water, drained
2 tablespoons light mayonnaise
8 slices low-carb wheat bread
4 slices fat-free sharp cheddar cheese

1. Preheat sprayed skillet over medium heat.

2. With fork in small mixing bowl, break up tuna into smaller flakes. Add mayonnaise and mix well.

3. On 4 slices of bread, spread tuna mixture and top with cheese and additional bread.

4. Place 1 sandwich in sprayed skillet and cook on one side until it browns. Spray top side of sandwich with cooking spray and cook that side until it browns.

5. Repeat with remaining 3 sandwiches. Serve warm.

Optional: Serve each sandwich with 1 large dill pickle.

Yield: *4 sandwiches*   Serving size: *1 sandwich*

Calories: *195*   Protein: *30 g*   Carbohydrate: *17 g*
Fat: *4 g*   Cholesterol: *23 mg*   Sodium: *873 mg*
Calcium: *2 mg*   Fiber: *4 g*   Sugars: *3 g*
Sugar Alcohol: *0 g*

Food Exchanges: *1 bread, 1 very lean meat, ½ fat*

■ ■ ■

Sauces

Green Chili Sauce
Net Carbs: 3 g

1 tablespoon regular stick margarine or butter
1½ tablespoons flour
1½ cups Swanson® Natural Goodness™ chicken broth
1 (4.5 ounce) can chopped green chiles, undrained

1. In heavy saucepan over medium heat, melt margarine.
   Add flour and stir until flour and butter mix well.
   When mixture bubbles, continue to cook and stir
   1 minute.

2. Gradually stir in broth and heat until it boils. Cook
   and stir 1 minute. Add green chiles and simmer 15 to
   20 minutes.

3. Use immediately or cover and chill for later use.

*Optional: Add ½ cup finely chopped onion and 1 finely minced
garlic clove to margarine before adding flour. Add
pinch ground cumin.*

Yield: 1½ cups   *Serving size: ¼ cup*

Calories: 31   *Protein: 1 g*   *Carbohydrate: 3 g*
Fat: 2 g   *Cholesterol: 0 mg*   *Sodium: 219 mg*
Calcium: 16 mg   *Fiber: less than 1 g*   *Sugars: less than 1 g*
Sugar Alcohol: 0 g

Food Exchanges: ½ fat

*To quickly chop an onion, slice off the stem and root
ends and remove peel. Halve the onion from top to
root end. Place each onion half flat side down and
make ¼-inch vertical slices. Holding the vertical slices
together, cut ¼-inch horizontal slices. There you go!*

Red Chili Enchilada Sauce

Net Carbs: 4 g

1 onion, finely chopped
2 cloves garlic, finely minced or pressed
3½ cups no-salt tomato sauce
2 to 4 tablespoons chili powder, divided

1. In sprayed large saucepan over medium heat, cook and stir onion and garlic 2 to 3 minutes or until onion is clear and tender.

2. Add tomato sauce and heat until it boils. Gradually stir in 2 tablespoons chili powder.

3. Reduce heat and simmer 15 minutes. Add additional chili powder to taste. Continue simmering at least 15 minutes, and season to taste with salt substitute.

4. Serve sauce as is or strain through wire mesh strainer. For smoother sauce, puree in food processor or blender. Refrigerate or freeze in small amounts for later use.

Optional: Add ½ teaspoon ground cumin and ¼ teaspoon crushed dried oregano.

Yield: 12 servings (About 3 cups)   *Serving size: ¼ cup*

Calories: 31   *Protein: 2 g*   *Carbohydrate: 6 g*
Fat: less than 1 g   *Cholesterol: 0 mg*   *Sodium: 35 mg*
Calcium: 30 mg   *Fiber: 2 g*   *Sugars: 5 g*
Sugar Alcohol: 0 g

Food Exchanges: ½ vegetable

■ ■ ■

Lower-Fat Pesto Spread

Net Carbs: less than 1 g

All the great flavors with much less fat!

1 tablespoon pine nuts
2 teaspoons dried basil leaves or 1½ teaspoons fresh chopped basil
¼ to ½ teaspoon finely minced garlic

1. In dry skillet over low heat, stir and toast pine nuts until they brown lightly. Do not burn.

2. Using wooden cutting board and rolling pin (or mortar and pestle), crush pine nuts. Add basil and garlic and mix well.

Optional: Add ¼ teaspoon olive oil.

Yield: About 1½ tablespoons Serving size: 2 teaspoons

Calories: 13	*Protein: less than 1 g*	*Carbohydrate: less than 1 g*
Fat: 1 g	*Cholesterol: 0 mg*	*Sodium: less than 1 g*
Calcium: 9 mg	*Fiber: less than 1 g*	*Sugars: 0 g*
Sugar Alcohol: 0 g		

Food Exchanges: 1 fat

■ ■ ■

Homemade Spaghetti Sauce
Net Carbs: 6 g

1 (12 ounce) package frozen seasoning blend (onions, celery,
    peppers, parsley)
2 cloves garlic, finely minced or pressed
3 cups no-salt tomato sauce
2 teaspoons Italian herb seasoning blend

1. In saucepan over medium heat, cook and stir seasoning
   blend, ¼ cup water and garlic until vegetables are
   tender.

2. Add tomato sauce and herb blend and heat until
   mixture boils. Reduce heat, cover and simmer 10 to
   15 minutes for flavors to blend.

Yield: 12 servings (About 3 cups)   *Serving size: About ¼ cup*

Calories: 30   *Protein: less than 1 g*   *Carbohydrate: 6 g*
Fat: 0 g   *Cholesterol: 0 mg*   *Sodium: 29 mg*
Calcium: less than 1 g   *Fiber: less than 1 g*   *Sugars: 5 g*
Sugar Alcohol: 0 g

Food Exchanges: ½ vegetable

■ ■ ■

Sweet and Sour Sauce

Net Carbs: 2 g

½ cup Splenda® sugar substitute
1 tablespoon corn starch
⅓ cup rice or white wine vinegar
1 tablespoon lite (reduced sodium) soy sauce

1. In medium saucepan, mix sugar substitute and corn starch.

2. Stir in ½ cup water, vinegar and soy sauce and mix well.

3. Over medium heat, heat mixture until it boils, stirring constantly. Boil and stir 1 minute.

4. Use sauce immediately or refrigerate.

Yield: 10 servings (About 1 cup)   *Serving size: 1 tablespoon*

Calories: 8   *Protein: less than 1 g*   *Carbohydrate: 2 g*
Fat: 0 g   *Cholesterol: 0 mg*   *Sodium: 58 mg*
Calcium: 1 mg   *Fiber: 0 g*   *Sugars: less than 1 g*
Sugar Alcohol: 0 g

Food Exchanges: 0

■ ■ ■

Spicy Tomato Sauce
Net Carbs: 7 g

1 clove garlic, finely minced
2 (8 ounce) cans no-salt tomato sauce
1 teaspoon dried basil, crushed
½ teaspoon dried oregano, crushed

1. In sprayed 1-quart saucepan over medium heat, cook and stir garlic about 1 minute. Do not burn. Add tomato sauce, basil, oregano and salt substitute and pepper to taste. Heat mixture until it boils, then reduce heat and simmer 5 to 6 minutes. Serve over reduced-carb or whole wheat pasta.

Yield: 4 servings (2 cups)   *Serving size: ½ cup*

Calories: 39   *Protein: 1 g*   *Carbohydrate: 8 g*
Fat: less than 1 g   *Cholesterol: 0 mg*   *Sodium: 37 mg*
Calcium: 5 mg   *Fiber: 1 g*   *Sugars: 7 g*
Sugar Alcohol: 0 g

Food Exchanges: ½ vegetable

■ ■ ■

◆

Good vegetable sources of vitamin C are tomatoes, peppers, broccoli, and cauliflower.

Easy-to-Make Cheese Sauce

Net Carbs: 7 g

2 tablespoons light butter
2 tablespoons all-purpose flour
1¼ cups skim milk
¼ cup shredded reduced-fat cheddar cheese

1. In heavy saucepan over medium heat, melt butter. Add flour, cook and stir about 2 minutes. Do not brown.

2. Stirring constantly, add milk and heat until it boils. Reduce heat and cook 2 to 3 minutes until sauce thickens.

3. Add cheese and stir until cheese melts. Remove from heat and serve immediately.

Tip: If not serving immediately, cover sauce with plastic wrap and chill.

Yield: 4 servings (about 1 cup)   *Serving size: ¼ cup*

Calories: 111   *Protein: 7 g*   *Carbohydrate: 7 g*
Fat: 7 g   *Cholesterol: 22 mg*   *Sodium: 180 mg*
Calcium: 172 mg   *Fiber: less than 1 g*   *Sugars: 4 g*
Sugar Alcohol: 0 g

Food Exchanges: 1 milk, 2 fat

■ ■ ■

Mustard Sauce
Net Carbs: 3 g

2 tablespoons Smart Balance® buttery spread
2 tablespoons quick-mixing or all-purpose flour
2 cups skim milk
2 to 4 tablespoons dijon-style, brown or Creole mustard

1. In saucepan over medium heat, melt buttery spread.
   Stir in flour and mix well.

2. Add milk, stirring constantly until mixture boils. Boil
   1 minute until mixture thickens and becomes smooth.

3. Remove from heat and stir in mustard. Serve hot or
   warm.

Yield: 16 servings (2 cups)   Serving size: 2 tablespoons

Calories: 27   *Protein: 2 g*   *Carbohydrate: 3 g*
Fat: 1 g   *Cholesterol: less than 1 mg*   *Sodium: 92 mg*
Calcium: 32 mg   *Dietary Fiber: less than 1 g* *Sugars: 2 g*
Sugar Alcohol: 0 g

Food Exchanges: 0

■ ■ ■

Stir-Fry Cooking Sauce

Net Carbs: 3 g

4 teaspoons corn starch
2 teaspoons lite (reduced sodium) soy sauce
½ teaspoon ground ginger
2 tablespoons cooking sherry or water

1. In small bowl, combine all ingredients and stir until corn starch dissolves. Stir again before using.

Yield: 4 servings (about 1 cup)   *Serving size: ¼ cup*

Calories: 18   *Protein: less than 1 g*   *Carbohydrate: 3 g*
Fat: 0 g   *Cholesterol: 0 mg*   *Sodium: 120 mg*
Calcium: 1 mg   *Fiber: less than 1 g*   *Sugars: less than 1 g*
Sugar Alcohol: 0 g

Food Exchanges: 0

■ ■ ■

Lemon Oil Dressing

Net Carbs: less than 1 g

¼ cup olive oil
1 teaspoon grated lemon peel and 2 to 3 tablespoons lemon juice
1 tablespoon chopped green onion with tops
¼ to ½ teaspoon garlic powder

1. In jar or container with lid, mix or shake all ingredients until they mix well.

2. Shake again before serving.

Yield: 8 servings (about ½ cup)   *Serving size: 1 tablespoon*

Calories: 61   *Protein: less than 1 g*   *Carbohydrate: less than 1 g*
Fat: 7 g   *Cholesterol: 0 mg*   *Sodium: 90 mg*
Calcium: 1 mg   *Fiber: less than 1 g*   *Sugars: less than 1 g*
Sugar Alcohol: 0 g

Food Exchanges: 1½ fat

■ ■ ■

Soy Sauce Dressing

Net Carbs: less than 1 g

4 teaspoons canola, peanut or olive oil
4 teaspoons white wine or rice vinegar
2 teaspoons lite (reduced sodium) soy sauce
1 teaspoon Splenda® sugar substitute

1. In small bowl, mix all ingredients.

2. Stir well before serving.

Yield: 9 servings (About 3 tablespoons)   *Serving size: About 1 teaspoon*

Calories: 19   *Protein: less than 1 g*   *Carbohydrate: less than 1 g*
Fat: 2 g   *Cholesterol: 0 mg*   *Sodium: 43 mg*
Calcium: less than 1 mg   *Fiber: 0 g*   *Sugars: less than 1 g*
Sugar Alcohol: 0 g

Food Exchanges: ½ fat

■ ■ ■

Desserts

Peach Lovers' Reward

Net Carbs: 16 g

1 (.3 ounce) package sugar-free peach gelatin mix
1 (15 ounce) can sliced peaches, reserve juice
1 (4 ounce) jar pureed peaches baby food
¼ teaspoon almond extract

1. In saucepan, heat 1 cup water until it boils. Add gelatin and stir until it dissolves.

2. Add juice from peaches and mix well. Stir in pureed peaches and sliced peaches and mix well. Pour into 1½-quart square dish. Chill about 4 hours or until gelatin sets.

Optional: Serve with lite or fat-free whipped topping.

Yield: 4 to 6 servings   *Serving size: ½ cup*

Calories: 75   *Protein: 1 g*   *Carbohydrate: 17 g*
Fat: less than 1 g   *Cholesterol: 0 mg*   *Sodium: 36 mg*
Calcium: 2 mg   *Fiber: 1 g*   *Sugars: 15 g*
Sugar Alcohol: 0 g

Food Exchanges: ½ fruit, ½ other carb

■ ■ ■

Super Melon-Berry Sundae
Net Carbs: 19 g

1 cup crushed fresh berries or unsweetened frozen berries, slightly
  thawed
1 to 2 tablespoons Splenda® sugar substitute
4 cups cubed melon (cantaloupe, honeydew)
2 cups low-carb vanilla ice cream

1. In mixing bowl, gently combine berries and sugar
   substitute. In each of 4 dessert bowls, place melon cubes
   and top with ½ cup ice cream. Top each sundae with
   ¼ cup berries and serve immediately.

Yield: 4 servings   *Serving size: 1 sundae*

Calories: 175   *Protein: 4 g*   *Carbohydrate: 29 g*
Fat: 6 g   *Cholesterol: 25 mg* *Sodium: 51 mg*
Calcium: 17 mg   *Fiber: 6 g*   *Sugars: 18 g*
Sugar Alcohol: 4 g

Food Exchanges: 1 fruit, 1 other carb

■ ■ ■

Special Kiwi Delight
Net Carbs: 11 g

3 large kiwi fruit
2 tablespoons Splenda® sugar substitute
1 cup lite or fat-free frozen whipped topping
⅛ teaspoon vanilla extract

1. Peel kiwi fruit. Cut 1 kiwi fruit crosswise in half and reserve 1 half for garnish. Cut remaining kiwi fruit into chunks.

2. In blender or food processor on medium speed, blend kiwi fruit and sugar substitute until smooth.

3. In mixing bowl, lightly mix blended kiwi fruit, whipped topping and vanilla extract.

4. Into 4 parfait or stemmed glasses, spoon kiwi fruit mixture and garnish with reserved kiwi fruit slices.

5. Chill before serving.

Variations: Substitute fresh peaches, strawberries or raspberries for kiwi fruit; substitute almond extract for vanilla extract.

Yield: 4 servings   *Serving size: ½ cup*

Calories: 80	*Protein: less than 1 g*	*Carbohydrate: 13 g*
Fat: 2 g	*Cholesterol: 0 mg*	*Sodium: 1 mg*
Calcium: 23 mg	*Fiber: 2 g*	*Sugars: 8 g*
Sugar Alcohol: 0 g		

Just 1 glazed doughnut equals 2 carbohydrate and 2 fat exchanges.

Bubbly Apple Crunch
Net Carbs: 12 g

1 (20 ounce) can lite no-sugar-added apple pie filling
20 Murray® sugar-free vanilla wafers
½ teaspoon ground cinnamon
¼ cup chopped pecans

1. Preheat oven to 300°.

2. Chop apple pie filling into small pieces.

3. Coarsely crush vanilla wafers. Stir cinnamon and pecans into crushed wafers.

4. Spray 6 ovenproof custard cups with butter-flavored, non-stick cooking spray. Spoon ¼ cup pie filling into each cup and sprinkle with 1 tablespoon wafer mixture. Spoon additional ¼ cup pie filling onto wafer mixture and top with 1 tablespoon wafer mixture.

5. Heat in oven at 300° for 20 minutes or until pie filling bubbles and heats through.

Yield: 6 servings   *Serving size: 1 custard cup*

Calories: 108   *Protein: 1 g*   *Carbohydrate: 16 g*
Fat: 5 g   *Cholesterol: 0 mg*   *Sodium: 35 mg*
Calcium: 5.5 mg   *Fiber: less than 1 g*   *Sugars: 6 g*
Sugar Alcohol: 3 g

Food Exchanges: 1 bread, 1 fat, ½ fruit

If a can of fruit is labeled "unsweetened," it means that no sugar has been added. Keep in mind there are natural sugars in the fruit.

Maple Syrup Stir-Fry Apples
Net Carbs: 8 g

2 unpeeled tart apples, cored, thinly sliced
1 to 2 tablespoons sugar-free maple or breakfast syrup

1. In sprayed skillet over medium heat, add apples and spray with non-stick cooking spray. Cook and stir apples until brown on both sides.

2. Add ¼ cup water, cover and simmer 10 to 15 minutes or until apples cook. Remove cover, increase heat to high and stir until water evaporates.

3. Serve apples warm with syrup.

Optional: If you don't want to use maple syrup, try 1 tablespoon Splenda® sugar substitute mixed with ½ teaspoon ground cinnamon.

Yield: 4 servings (about 1 cup)   *Serving size: ¼ cup*

Calories: 37   *Protein: less than 1 g*   *Carbohydrate: 10 g*
Fat: less than 1 g   *Cholesterol: 0 mg*   *Sodium: 2 mg*
Calcium: 4 mg   *Fiber: 2 g*   *Sugars: 7 g*
Sugar Alcohol: less than 1 g

Food Exchanges: ½ fruit

■ ■ ■

Summertime Melon Supreme
Net Carbs: 14 g

1 large lime
4 tablespoons Splenda® sugar substitute
¼ teaspoon ground ginger
4 cups cubed watermelon, honeydew or cantaloupe

1. Grate 1 tablespoon lime peel and squeeze 4 teaspoons fresh lime juice.

2. In saucepan, mix ½ cup water, lime juice, sugar substitute and ginger. Heat just until mixture begins to boil. Remove from heat and cool to room temperature.

3. Into each of 4 dessert bowls, place 1 cup melon cubes. Drizzle with lime juice mixture.

4. Garnish with grated lime peel and serve.

Yield: 4 servings   *Serving size: 1 cup melon with syrup*

Calories: 47   *Protein: less than 1 g*   *Carbohydrate: 14 g*
Fat: less than 1 g   *Cholesterol: 0 mg*   *Sodium: 2 mg*
Calcium: 11 mg   *Fiber: less than 1 g*   *Sugars: 10 g*
Sugar Alcohol: 0 mg

Food Exchanges: 1 fruit

■ ■ ■

Down-Home Stewed Apples
Net Carbs: 24 g

6 firm, mildly tart Granny Smith, Gala or Jonathan apples
⅔ cup water or unsweetened apple juice
2 teaspoons ground cinnamon or 1 large cinnamon stick
2 tablespoons Splenda® sugar substitute

1. Peel and core apples. Cut in ½-inch thick slices.

2. In large heavy skillet or saucepan, place apples and add water and ground cinnamon.

3. Cover and simmer, stirring frequently, over low heat about 20 minutes or until apples are tender but not mushy.

4. Stir in sugar substitute and mix until it dissolves, about 1 minute. Remove from heat. Serve warm.

Yield: About 4 servings   *Serving size: ½ cup*

Calories: 111   *Protein: less than 1 g*   *Carbohydrate: 30 g*
Fat: less than 1 g   *Cholesterol: 0 mg*   *Sodium: 2 mg*
Calcium: 27 mg   *Fiber: 6 g*   *Sugars: 22 g*
Sugar Alcohol: 0 g

Food Exchanges: 2 fruit

◆

Many canned and bottled juices are loaded with sugar and calories. Look for "no sugar added" and "unsweetened" varieties.

Angel Pistachio-Strawberry Trifle

Net Carbs: 16 g

2 (1 ounce) packages sugar-free instant pistachio pudding mix
4 cups skim milk
1 prepared strawberry sugar-free angel food cake
3 cups sliced fresh strawberries, slightly crushed

1. In mixing bowl, combine pudding mix and milk and mix well. Tear cake into bite-size pieces.

2. In trifle bowl or large clear glass bowl, place ⅓ cake pieces in single layer. Spoon ¼ pudding over cake, followed by 1 cup strawberries.

3. Repeat layers twice, ending with strawberries on top.

4. Chill before serving.

Optional: Garnish each serving with 2 tablespoons lite or fat-free whipped topping.

Yield: 10 to 12 servings   *Serving size: ¾ cup*

Calories: 113   *Protein: 5 g*   *Carbohydrate: 26 g*
Fat: less than 1 g   *Cholesterol: 2 mg*   *Sodium: 463 mg*
Calcium: 87 mg   *Fiber: 1 g*   *Sugars: 6 g*
Sugar Alcohol: 9 g

Food Exchanges: 1 bread, ½ fruit, ½ milk

Store fresh strawberries in the refrigerator in a shallow container covered with plastic wrap. Use within 3 days.

Guiltless Fruit Parfait

Net Carbs: 14 g

2 (6 ounce) cartons low-carb vanilla yogurt
1 to 3 tablespoons sugar-free fruit drink powder
2 cups mixed fresh fruit*
4 tablespoons lite or fat-free frozen whipped topping, thawed

1. In mixing bowl, combine yogurt and drink powder to taste.

2. Into 4 parfait or stemmed glasses, layer ¼ cup yogurt, 2 tablespoons fruit, ¼ cup yogurt and 2 tablespoons fruit.

3. Top each dessert with 1 tablespoon whipped topping before serving.

Tip: Strawberry and fruit punch drink powders are really good. Strawberries, apples, peaches, and blueberries are terrific. If you use fruit that browns easily such as peaches and bananas, serve immediately or sprinkle fruit with fruit preservative.

Yield: 4 servings   *Serving size: 1¼ cups*

Calories: 97   *Protein: 4 g*   *Carbohydrate: 16 g*
Fat: less than 1 g   *Cholesterol: 0 mg*   *Sodium: 61 mg*
Calcium: 9 mg   *Fiber: 2 g*   *Sugars: 10 g*
Sugar Alcohol: 0 g

Food Exchanges: ½ fruit, ½ skim milk

■ ■ ■

Poached Pears with Raspberry Sauce

Net Carbs: 18 g

½ cup Splenda® sugar substitute
Cinnamon stick
2 whole ripe pears, peeled, halved, cored
2 tablespoons 100% seedless raspberry spreadable fruit

1. In small saucepan, heat and stir 2 cups water, sugar substitute and cinnamon stick until water boils. Using slotted spoon, add pears to boiling syrup. Reduce heat to simmer.

2. Simmer pears 6 to 7 minutes or until they are tender. With slotted spoon, transfer each pear to dessert plate.

3. In custard cup, combine 1 tablespoon water and fruit spread. Microwave on HIGH about 15 seconds.

4. Drizzle 2 teaspoons fruit spread on each pear half. Serve warm.

Yield: 4 servings   *Serving size: ½ pear*

Calories: 68   *Protein: less than 1 g*   *Carbohydrate: 21 g*
Fat: less than 1 g   *Cholesterol: 0 mg*   *Sodium: less than 1 mg*
Calcium: 7 mg   *Fiber: 3 g*   *Sugars: 12 g*
Sugar Alcohol: 0 g

Food Exchanges: 1 fruit

■ ■ ■

⅔ White Chocolate-Strawberry Trifle

Net Carbs: 16 g

2 (1 ounce) packages sugar-free instant white chocolate pudding
   mix
4 cups skim milk
4 cups sliced fresh strawberries
1 (8 ounce) carton frozen strawberry whipped topping, thawed

1. In mixing bowl, combine pudding mix and milk and
   mix well.

2. In 2-quart glass bowl or trifle bowl, spread 2 cups
   pudding and 2 cups sliced strawberries. Repeat layers.
   Spoon strawberry whipped topping on top. Serve
   immediately or chill.

Yield: 10 to 12 servings   *Serving size: ½ cup*

Calories: 125   *Protein: 3 g*   *Carbohydrate: 17 g*
Fat: 4 g   *Cholesterol: 0 mg*   *Sodium: 291 mg*
Calcium: 117 mg   *Fiber: 1 g*   *Sugars: 9 g*
Sugar Alcohol: 0 g

Food Exchanges: 1 fat, ½ fruit, ½ milk

■ ■ ■

Chilled Cappuccino Parfait
Net Carbs: 21 g

1 (1 ounce) package sugar-free instant vanilla pudding mix
½ cup strong brewed regular or decaffeinated coffee, chilled
1½ cups skim milk
2 cups lite frozen whipped topping, thawed

1. In mixing bowl, combine pudding mix, coffee and milk and mix well.

2. Into stemmed or parfait glasses, layer 1 to 2 tablespoons pudding and 1 to 2 tablespoons whipped topping. Repeat layers twice.

3. Chill before serving.

Yield: 4 servings   *Serving size: About ½ cup*

Calories: 145   *Protein: 3 g*   *Carbohydrate: 21 g*
Fat: 4 g   *Cholesterol: 2 mg*   *Sodium: 480 mg*
Calcium: 84 mg   *Fiber: 0 g*   *Sugars: 9 g*
Sugar Alcohol: 0 g

Food Exchanges: 1 bread, 1 fat, ½ milk

■ ■ ■

Valentine's Sweetheart Dessert
Net Carbs: 7 g

1½ cups low-carb or no-sugar-added strawberry yogurt
1 to 2 tablespoons Splenda® sugar substitute
Few drops red food coloring, if desired
2 cups halved or sliced fresh strawberries

1. In mixing bowl, combine yogurt and sugar substitute and mix well. If desired, add few drops red food coloring. Into 4 dessert dishes, place strawberries and spoon yogurt mixture on top.

Tip: This is very delicious with frozen unsweetened strawberries, partially thawed, if you cannot get fresh strawberries.

Yield: 4 servings   *Serving size: ½ cup*

Calories: 68   *Protein: 5 g*   *Carbohydrate: 8 g*
Fat: 2 g   *Cholesterol: 8 mg*   *Sodium: 36 mg*
Calcium: 12 mg   *Fiber: 1 g*   *Sugars: 6 g*
Sugar Alcohol: 0 g

Food Exchanges: ½ fruit, ½ fat

■ ■ ■

Angel Food Chocolate Sundae

Net Carbs: 26 g

½ prepared sugar-free unfrosted angel food cake
1½ cups frozen lite whipped topping, thawed
4 tablespoons sugar-free, fat-free chocolate syrup
¾ cup chopped Russell Stover® low-carb toffee squares or other
low-carb candy

1. For each dessert, cut or tear 2½-inch slice from angel
food cake. Place on dessert plate and mound with
whipped topping.

2. Drizzle whipped topping with chocolate syrup. Spoon
2 to 3 teaspoons candy on top and serve immediately.

Yield: 4 servings   *Serving size: 1 (2½-inch) slice cake with toppings*

Calories: 228   *Protein: 3 g*   *Carbohydrate: 44 g*
Fat: 7 g   *Cholesterol: 5 mg*   *Sodium: 319 mg*
Calcium: 10 mg   *Fiber: less than 1 g*   *Sugars: 3 g*
Sugar Alcohol: 18 g

Food Exchanges: 2 bread, 1 fat, 1 other carb

■ ■ ■

Sweet Cherry Cobbler
Net Carbs: 11 g

1 (20 ounce) can lite no-sugar-added cherry pie filling
2 to 3 tablespoons Splenda® sugar substitute
½ to 1 teaspoon almond extract
1 (9 inch) refrigerated piecrust

1. Preheat oven to 425°.

2. In mixing bowl, combine pie filling, sugar substitute and almond flavoring. Pour into 11 x 7 x 2-inch rectangular baking pan.

3. Unfold piecrust onto flat surface. Cut 4 (11 x 1-inch) strips from piecrust. Arrange strips lengthwise over pie filling. Cut 4 (7 x 1-inch) strips and arrange crosswise on pie filling.

4. Bake 25 minutes.

Optional: *Sprinkle leftover piecrust with cinnamon and sugar (or sugar substitute) and bake with cobbler. Kids will love it!*

Variation: *If you like apples, try 1 (20 ounce) can lite no-sugar-added apple pie filling instead of cherry pie filling and substitute ½ to 1 teaspoon ground cinnamon for almond flavoring. You have another fabulous dessert.*

Yield: About 10 servings   *Serving size: ½ cup*
Calories: 90   *Protein: less than 1 g*   *Carbohydrate: 11 g*
Fat: 5 g   *Cholesterol: 0 mg*   *Sodium: 73 mg*
Calcium: 1 mg   *Fiber: less than 1 g*   *Sugars: 4 g*
Sugar Alcohol: 0 g   *Food Exchanges: 1 fat, ½ bread*

■ ■ ■

Holiday Pumpkin Flan

Net Carbs: 18 g

1 (3 ounce) package flan mix with caramel packet
1½ cups skim milk
1 cup canned pumpkin
⅛ teaspoon pumpkin pie spice

1. Into 4 custard cups, pour equal amounts caramel sauce.

2. In saucepan, prepare flan mix according to package directions using 1½ cups milk. After mixture boils, remove saucepan from heat and stir in pumpkin and pumpkin pie spice.

3. Slowly pour equal amounts of mixture into each custard cup. Chill covered 1 to 2 hours.

4. When ready to serve, use table knife to loosen custard. Invert each custard cup onto small dessert plate so caramel sauce covers custard.

Optional: Garnish each dessert with whipped topping.

Yield: 4 servings   Serving size: ½ cup

Calories: 84   Protein: 3 g   Carbohydrate: 19 g
Fat: less than 1 g   Cholesterol: 1 mg   Sodium: 90 mg
Calcium: 70 mg   Fiber: 1 g   Sugars: 4 g
Sugar Alcohol: 0 g

Food Exchanges, 1 milk, ½ other carb

The higher the fat content of milk, the greater the amount of saturated fat and cholesterol.

Sugar-Free Egg Custard
Net Carbs: 9 g

A smooth as silk, satisfying custard dessert

1¾ cups fat-free milk
½ cup Splenda® sugar substitute
1 teaspoon vanilla
1 cup Egg Beaters® egg substitute

1. Preheat oven to 350°. In saucepan over medium heat, heat milk just to boiling. Remove from heat and whisk in sugar substitute and vanilla. Continue to whisk while gradually adding egg substitute. Pour into 4 sprayed custard cups.

2. Place custard cups in baking pan filled with 1 inch hot water. Bake 35 minutes or until knife inserted in center of custard comes out clean. Serve warm or chilled.

Tip: Sprinkle custards with nutmeg before baking.

Yield: 4 servings   Serving size: ½ cup

Calories: 69   Protein: 10 g   Carbohydrate: 9 g
Fat: 0 g   Cholesterol: 2 mg   Sodium: 162 mg
Calcium: 118 mg   Fiber: 0 g   Sugars: 6 g
Sugar Alcohol: 0 g

Food Exchanges: ½ milk, 1 very lean meat

■ ■ ■

⅋ Chocolate Cookie-Crumb Delight
Net Carbs: 18 g

2 cups skim milk
1 (1.5 ounce) package sugar-free instant chocolate pudding mix
1 (6.5 ounce) package Murray® sugar-free chocolate sandwich
cookies, coarsely crushed
1 (8 ounce) carton lite frozen whipped topping, thawed

1. In mixing bowl, combine milk and pudding mix and stir well.

2. In bottom of 11 x 7 x 1½-inch rectangular glass dish, spread cookies and set aside ¼ cup for garnish.

3. Spoon pudding evenly over cookies.

4. Spread whipped topping over pudding and garnish with reserved cookies.

5. Cover with plastic wrap and refrigerate before serving.

Optional: Double or triple this recipe for a crowd-pleasing favorite! To reduce net carbs, prepare with low-carb milk.

Variation: Substitute Murray® sugar-free shortbread cookies and butterscotch pudding mix or Murray® sugar-free vanilla wafers and banana cream pudding mix.

Yield: 10 servings	*Serving size: About ⅓ cup*	
Calories: 153	*Protein: 3 g*	*Carbohydrate: 21 g*
Fat: 7 g	*Cholesterol: less than 1 mg*	*Sodium: 215 mg*
Calcium: 45 mg	*Fiber: less than 1 g*	*Sugars: 5 g*
Sugar Alcohol: 3 g	*Food Exchanges: 1 bread, 1½ fat, ½ other carb*	

Old-Fashion Banana Pudding
Net Carbs: 29 g

2 (1 ounce) packages sugar-free instant vanilla pudding mix
4 cups skim milk
3 bananas
1 (6.5 ounce) package Murray® sugar-free vanilla wafers

1. In mixing bowl, combine pudding mix and milk and mix well.

2. Slice bananas.

3. Reserve 5 cookies for garnish and spread remaining vanilla wafers in 1 layer in 9 x 9-inch or 7 x 11-inch dish. Spoon 2 cups vanilla pudding over wafers and layer half banana slices over pudding.

4. Spread another layer of vanilla wafers and remaining banana slices. Spoon on remaining 2 cups vanilla pudding.

5. Crush reserved cookies and sprinkle over dessert. Chill 3 to 4 hours before serving.

Optional: To reduce net effective carbs, prepare with reduced-carb milk.

Yield: 8 to 10 servings   *Serving size: ½ cup*

Calories: 203   *Protein: 6 g*   *Carbohydrate: 36 g*
Fat: 4 g   *Cholesterol: 0 mg*   *Sodium: 439 mg*
Calcium: 135 mg   *Fiber: 1 g*   *Sugars: 10 g*
Sugar Alcohol: 6 g

Food Exchanges: 1 bread, 1 fruit, 1 fat, ½ milk

■ ■ ■

4-Layer Chocolate Delight
Net Carbs: 15 g

½ (8 ounce) package reduced-fat cream cheese (Neufchatel)
1 (1.5 ounce) package sugar-free instant chocolate pudding mix
2 cups skim milk
8 (2 inch square) chocolate graham crackers

1. In mixing bowl, beat cream cheese with electric mixer or wire whisk until it is very smooth.

2. In separate bowl, combine pudding mix and milk and mix well.

3. Add pudding to cream cheese and gently stir or swirl to mix.

4. In each of 4 dessert bowls, crumble 1 chocolate graham cracker. Spoon ½ cup pudding mixture on crumbs. Crumble additional graham cracker on top.

5. Cover and chill before serving.

Variation: Substitute 8 Murray® sugar-free chocolate sandwich cookies for graham crackers.

Yield: 4 to 5 servings   *Serving size: ½ cup*

Calories: 149   *Protein: 7 g*   *Carbohydrate: 15 g*
Fat: 6 g   *Cholesterol: 18 mg*   *Sodium: 465 mg*
Calcium: 144 mg   *Fiber: less than 1 g*   *Sugars: 7 g*
Sugar Alcohol: 0 g

Food Exchanges: 1 bread, 1 fat, ½ other carb

◆

Sugar-free puddings and gelatins are an excellent and inexpensive way to satisfy a sweet tooth.

Mandarin Orange Heaven

Net Carbs: 16 g

1 (1 ounce) package sugar-free instant vanilla pudding mix
1½ cups skim milk
½ teaspoon orange or almond extract
1 (11 ounce) can mandarin oranges, drained

1. In mixing bowl, combine pudding mix and milk and stir well.

2. Stir in almond or orange extract.

3. Carefully fold mandarin oranges into pudding. Spoon into 4 custard cups, parfait glasses or stemmed glasses. Chill before serving.

Variation: *To use as pie filling, pour prepared pudding into 1 (6 ounce) reduced-fat graham cracker crust. Top with lite whipped topping and chill before serving.*

Yield: 4 servings   *Serving size: ½ cup*

Calories: 76   *Protein: 3 g*   *Carbohydrate: 16 g*
Fat: less than 1 g   *Cholesterol: 2 mg*   *Sodium: 336 mg*
Calcium: 90 mg   *Fiber: less than 1 g*   *Sugars: 10 g*
Sugar Alcohol: 0 g

Food Exchanges: ½ fruit, ½ milk

◆

When counting portion sizes for canned fruit, count on the fruit with a small amount of juice.

Cherry-Almond Tapioca Crunch
Net Carbs: 20 g

1 (3 ounce) package fat-free tapioca pudding mix
2 cups skim milk
1 (20 ounce) can lite cherry pie filling
⅓ cup slivered almonds, toasted

1. Prepare tapioca with skim milk according to package directions. Be prepared to cook and stir mixture over medium heat about 15 minutes (have this cookbook handy to look through while you are stirring). After tapioca boils, remove from heat, let stand 15 minutes and stir twice.

2. Pour tapioca into 9 x 9-inch dish or into 4 individual custard cups. Cover with plastic wrap and chill about 30 minutes.

3. After tapioca thickens to pudding consistency, spoon cherry pie filling on top and sprinkle with almonds.

4. Chill again before serving.

Optional: Stir 2 to 3 tablespoons Splenda® sugar substitute and ½ teaspoon almond extract into cherry pie filling before spreading on tapioca.

Yield: 8 servings (about 4 cups)   *Serving size: ½ cup*

Calories: 117   *Protein: 3 g*   *Carbohydrate: 20 g*
Fat: 3 g   *Cholesterol: 1 mg*   *Sodium: 80 mg*
Calcium: 70 mg   *Fiber: less than 1 g*   *Sugars: 0 g*
Sugar Alcohol: 0 g

Food Exchanges: 1 fruit, ½ fat, ½ milk

■ ■ ■

Lemon Meringue Pudding Cups

Net Carbs: 17 g

¼ cup corn starch
1½ cups Splenda® sugar substitute, divided
2 eggs, separated
2 tablespoons fresh lemon juice

1. Preheat oven to 350°.

2. In saucepan over medium heat, mix corn starch and 1¼ cups sugar substitute. Gradually stir in 1½ cups cold water and stir until smooth.

3. Slightly beat egg yolks and stir into corn starch mixture. Stirring constantly, heat mixture until it boils and continue to boil 1 minute.

4. Remove from heat and stir in lemon juice and dash salt. Spoon into 4 ovenproof custard cups.

5. With electric mixer at high speed, beat 2 egg whites. When whites foam, gradually add ¼ cup sugar substitute and beat until soft white peaks form. Mound meringue in peaks on top of pudding.

6. Bake at 350° for 15 minutes or until meringue turns golden brown.

Yield: 4 servings   *Serving size: 1 custard cup*

Calories: 69   *Protein: 3 g*   *Carbohydrate: 17 g*
Fat: 2 g   *Cholesterol: 106 mg*   *Sodium: 36 mg*
Calcium: 14 mg   *Fiber: less than 1 g* *Sugars: less than 1 g*
Sugar Alcohol: 0 g

Food Exchanges: 1 bread

■ ■ ■

❧ Pumpkin Pie In-A-Flash

Net Carbs: 12 g

This is so easy for a pie or pudding. Bake a 9-inch prepared piecrust for this quick recipe or pour filling into 8 custard cups for a pudding dessert.

1 cup canned pumpkin puree
3 cups skim milk
2 (.9 ounce) packages sugar-free cook-and-serve vanilla
    pudding mix
1 teaspoon pumpkin pie spice

1. Measure pumpkin to have ready before cooking pudding.

2. In heavy medium saucepan over medium heat, pour milk and stir in pudding mix and pumpkin pie spice. Cook over medium heat, stirring constantly, until mixture comes to full boil. Mixture will be thick.

3. Remove from heat and immediately stir in pumpkin.

Optional: For garnish, top pudding with mixture of 1½ cups lite frozen whipped topping and ½ teaspoon orange extract or 1 teaspoon finely grated orange peel.

Yield: 8 servings   *Serving size: ⅛ of pie*
Calories: 61   *Protein: 3 g*   *Carbohydrate: 12 g*
Fat: less than 1 g   *Cholesterol: 2 mg*   *Sodium: 151 mg*
Calcium: 93 mg   *Fiber: less than 1 g*   *Sugars: 10 g*
Sugar Alcohol: 0 g
Food Exchanges: ½ bread

◆

In this recipe, be sure to use regular canned pumpkin, not pumpkin pie mix, which contains added sugar.

Toffee Candy Pie
Net Carbs: 10 g

1 (8 ounce) carton lite frozen whipped topping, thawed
1 (1 ounce) package sugar-free instant butterscotch pudding mix
2½ cups low-carb vanilla ice cream, softened
3 (1 ounce) packages Russell Stover® low-carb toffee squares,
   frozen, coarsely chopped

1. In mixing bowl, combine whipped topping and pudding mix.

2. Add ice cream and mix well.

3. Reserve about 1 tablespoon chopped candy for garnish and fold remaining candy into pudding mix.

4. Spoon pie into 1 (6 ounce) graham cracker crust, garnish with reserved candy and freeze.

5. Remove pie from freezer about 10 minutes before serving.

Yield: 8 servings (1 pie)   *Serving size: ⅛ pie*

Calories *(without crust)*: 178   Protein: 2 g   Carbohydrate: 21 g
Fat: 10 g   Cholesterol: 19 mg   Sodium: 191 mg
Calcium: 0 mg   Fiber: 3 g   Sugars: 4 g
Sugar Alcohol: 8 g

Food Exchanges: 2 fat, 1½ other carb

◆

*Low-carb candies and chocolates are a
special treat now widely available.
Remember to watch portion sizes and calories.*

Lime Cheesecake You'll Love
Net Carbs: 9 g

2 cups low-fat small curd cottage cheese
1 (8 ounce) package reduced-fat cream cheese (Neufchatel)
1 cup Splenda® sugar substitute
3 to 4 limes

1. In wire mesh strainer over large bowl, spoon cottage cheese and set in refrigerator to drain 30 minutes.

2. Preheat oven to 350° and remove upper oven rack.

3. Transfer well drained cottage cheese to food processor or electric mixer, and beat until very smooth. Add cream cheese and beat again until mixture is smooth.

4. Grate 4 teaspoons lime peel, and squeeze 2 tablespoons lime juice. Add sugar substitute, 2 teaspoons lime peel and lime juice to cream cheese mixture. Mix thoroughly.

5. In lightly sprayed 8-inch springform pan, pour mixture. Place pan on large piece aluminum foil and carefully fold foil up over edges of pan so water will not leak into pan.

6. Set springform pan in large baking dish with sides and pour very hot or boiling water into baking dish until water reaches halfway up sides of springform pan.

7. Transfer pans to lower or middle oven rack and bake at 350° for about 45 minutes or until edges of cheesecake puff, but center is still moist. Cool completely before removing from pan. Garnish with reserved lime peel and serve.

Yield: 6 servings   *Serving size: ⅙ cheesecake*
Calories: 161   *Protein: 13 g*   *Carbohydrate: 9 g*
Fat: 10 g   *Cholesterol: 32 mg*   *Sodium: 395 mg*
Calcium: 85 mg   *Sodium: 395 mg*   *Calcium: 85 mg*
Fiber: less than 1 g   *Sugars: less than 1 g* *Sugar Alcohol: 0 g*
Food Exchanges: 1 medium fat meat

Creamy Peanut Butter Bites

Net Carbs: 3 g

¼ cup Carb Options™ creamy peanut spread
1½ tablespoons Splenda® sugar substitute
1 tablespoon nonfat dry milk powder
2 to 3 tablespoons chopped dry roasted unsalted peanuts

1. In small bowl, mix peanut spread, sugar substitute and milk powder. Form mixture into 1-inch balls and add few drops water if needed. Roll balls in chopped peanuts. Serve immediately or chill.

Yield: About 10 (1 inch) balls   *Serving size: 2 balls*

Calories: 106   *Protein: 4 g*   *Carbohydrate: 4 g*
Fat: 9 g   *Cholesterol: less than 1 mg*   *Sodium: 57 mg*
Calcium: 13 mg   *Fiber: 1 g*   *Sugars: 1 g*
Sugar Alcohol: 0 g

Food Exchanges: 2 fat

■ ■ ■

Sugar-Free Cookie Piecrust
Net Carbs: 18 g

1½ cups fine crumbs of Murray® sugar-free vanilla wafers
⅓ cup Smart Balance® buttery spread, melted

1. Preheat oven to 350°. In mixing bowl, combine cookie crumbs and buttery spread and mix well. In 8-inch pie plate, pat crumbs evenly.

2. Bake at 350° for 10 minutes, remove from oven and cool. Fill crust with no-bake pie filling of your choice. Chill as needed until pie filling sets.

Yield: 8 servings   *Serving size: ⅛ crust*

Calories: 229   *Protein: 3 g*   *Carbohydrate: 28 g*
Fat: 13 g   *Cholesterol: 0 mg*   *Sodium: 199 mg*
Calcium: 0 mg   *Fiber: 0 g*   *Sugars: 0 g*
Sugar Alcohol: 10 g

Food Exchanges: 2½ fat, 2 bread

■ ■ ■

Yummy Graham Cracker Piecrust

Net Carbs: 33 g

1½ cup crumbs of plain graham cracker crumbs
2 tablespoons Splenda® sugar substitute
⅓ cup Smart Balance® buttery spread, melted

1. Preheat oven to 350°. In mixing bowl, combine graham cracker crumbs and sugar substitute and mix well. Stir in buttery spread and mix.

2. In 9-inch pie plate, pat crumbs evenly.

3. Bake at 350° for 10 minutes, remove from oven and cool.

4. Fill crust with no-bake pie filling of your choice. Chill as needed until pie filling sets.

Yield: 8 servings   *Serving size: ⅛ crust*

Calories: 233   *Protein: 3 g*   *Carbohydrate: 33 g*
Fat: 10 g   *Cholesterol: 0 mg*   *Sodium: 317 mg*
Calcium: 10 mg   *Fiber: less than 1 g*   *Sugars: 13 g*
Sugar Alcohol: 0 g

Food Exchanges: 2 bread, 2 fat

■ ■ ■

Lemon-Zest Cheesecake

Net Carbs: 11 g

2 cups part-skim ricotta cheese, drained
1 (8 ounce) package reduced-fat cream cheese (Neufchatel)
1 cup Splenda® sugar substitute
1 lemon

1. Preheat oven to 350°. In food processor or electric mixer, beat ricotta cheese until very smooth. Add cream cheese and beat well.

3. Grate 2 tablespoons lemon peel and squeeze 1 tablespoon lemon juice. Add sugar substitute, lemon juice and grated peel to cream cheese mixture and mix thoroughly.

4. Pour mixture into sprayed 8-inch springform pan. Form aluminum foil from bottom to top of pan to prevent water leaks. Place pan in larger baking dish and pour very hot or boiling water in larger dish until water reaches halfway up springform pan.

5. Place pans carefully in oven and bake 45 minutes or until cheesecake puffs slightly. Cheesecake is done when table knife is inserted into middle of cheesecake and comes out clean.

Optional: Serve with fresh crushed strawberries.

Variation: For a little different flavor, substitute 2 cups well drained cottage cheese for ricotta cheese. Substitute 2 teaspoons vanilla for lemon juice and zest.

Yield: 6 servings
Calories: 201
Fat: 13 g
Calcium: 266 mg
Sugar Alcohol: 0 g

Serving size: ⅙ cheesecake
Protein: 13 g   Carbohydrate: 11 g
Cholesterol: 47 mg   Sodium: 214 mg
Fiber: less than 1 g   Sugars: less than 1 g
Food Exchanges: 1 medium fat meat, ½ fat

Nutty Hot Fudge Ice Cream Pie
Net Carbs: 11 g
Tastes like an old-fashion ice cream bar!

3 cups low-carb vanilla ice cream, softened
1 (8 ounce) carton lite frozen whipped topping, thawed
⅓ cup chopped mixed nut ice cream topping
Smuckers® Sugar-Free Hot Fudge Topping™

1. In mixing bowl, combine ice cream and whipped topping and mix well.

2. Spoon mixture into 1 (6 ounce) graham cracker crust and sprinkle nuts evenly over top.

3. Heat hot fudge topping according to directions on jar, drizzle over pie and freeze.

4. Remove from freezer about 10 minutes before serving.

Variation: Substitute low-carb chocolate, low-carb strawberry or low-carb mint ice cream for vanilla ice cream.

Yield: 8 servings (filling for 1 pie)   *Serving size: 1 slice (⅛ pie)*

Calories (without crust): 186   Protein: 3 g   Carbohydrate: 18 g
Fat: 10 g   Cholesterol: 19 mg   Sodium: 40 mg
Calcium: 0 mg   Fiber: 3 g   Sugars: 5 g
Sugar Alcohol: 4 g

"Low carb" does not always been "low calorie." Check the food label.

Chocolate Cream Pie
Net Carbs: 8 g

4 ounces reduced fat-cream cheese (Neufchatel), softened
1 (1.5 ounce) package sugar-free instant chocolate pudding mix
2 cups skim milk
¼ cup chopped pecans, toasted

1. In mixing bowl, beat cream cheese with electric mixer or wire whisk until very smooth.

2. In separate bowl, combine pudding mix and milk and mix well.

3. Add pudding to cream cheese and gently stir or swirl to mix. Fold in pecans.

4. Spoon mixture into 1 (6 ounce) graham cracker crust.

5. Cover and chill before serving.

Optional: Top with mixture of 1½ cups lite whipped topping and 1 tablespoon miniature chocolate chips or chopped sugar-free chocolate.

Yield: 8 servings   *Serving size: ⅛ of pie*

Calories (without crust): 97   *Protein: 4 g*   *Carbohydrate: 8 g*
Fat: 6 g   *Cholesterol: 12 g*   *Sodium: 242 mg*
Calcium: 69 mg   *Fiber: less than 1 g*   *Sugars: 3 g*
Sugar Alcohol: 0 g

Food Exchanges: 1 fat, ½ bread, ½ milk

■ ■ ■

Peanut Butter Cup Pie
Net Carbs: 11 g

½ cup Smuckers® natural creamy peanut butter
2 cups low-carb vanilla ice cream, softened
1 (8 ounce) carton lite frozen whipped topping, thawed
3 (1.2 ounce) packages Russell Stover® low-carb peanut butter
   cups, frozen, coarsely chopped

1. In mixing bowl, combine peanut butter and ice cream and mix well.

2. Add whipped topping and mix.

3. Reserve about ¼ cup candy for garnish and fold remaining candy into peanut butter mixture.

4. Spoon pie into 1 (6 ounce) graham cracker crust, garnish with reserved candy and freeze.

5. Remove from freezer about 10 minutes before serving.

Yield: 8 servings (1 pie)   *Serving size: 1 slice (⅛ pie)*

Calories (without crust): 282   *Protein: 7 g*   *Carbohydrate: 21 g*
Fat: 19 g   *Cholesterol: 14 mg*   *Sodium: 114 mg*
Calcium: 0 mg   *Fiber: 3 g*   *Sugars: 5 g*
Sugar Alcohol: 7 g

Food Exchanges: 4 fat, 1½ other carb

To make chopping easier, freeze chocolate bars and other chocolate candy before beginning recipe preparation.

Mom's Banana Cream Pie

Net Carbs: 12 g

1 (.9 ounce) package sugar-free instant banana cream pudding mix
1½ cups skim milk
1 (8 ounce) carton lite frozen whipped topping, thawed, divided
2 tablespoons flaked coconut, toasted

1. In mixing bowl, combing pudding mix and milk and mix well. Fold in 2 cups whipped topping and mix.

2. Pour mixture into 1 (6 ounce) graham cracker crust. Sprinkle toasted coconut on top and chill pie until pudding sets.

Yield: 8 servings   *Serving size: 1 slice (⅛ pie)*

Calories (without crust): 97   *Protein: 2 g*   *Carbohydrate: 12 g*
Fat: 4 g   *Cholesterol: less than 1 g*   *Sodium: 153 mg*
Calcium: 42 mg   *Fiber: less than 1 g*   *Sugars: 6 g*
Sugar Alcohol: 0 g

Food Exchanges: 1 fat, ½ bread

■ ■ ■

Chocolate Mint Ice Cream Pie

Net Carbs: 14 g

3½ cups low-carb mint chip ice cream, softened
1 teaspoon peppermint extract
1 (8 ounce) carton lite frozen whipped topping
8 Murray® sugar-free chocolate sandwich cookies, crushed

1. In mixing bowl, combine ice cream and peppermint extract. Fold in whipped topping and mix well.

2. Spoon filling into 1 (6 ounce) chocolate graham cracker crust, garnish with crushed cookies and freeze. Remove from freezer about 10 minutes before serving.

Yield: 8 servings (1 pie)   *Serving size: ⅛ pie*

Calories: 199   *Protein: 2 g*   *Carbohydrate: 23 g*
Fat: 12 g   *Cholesterol: 22 mg*   *Sodium: 37 mg*
Calcium: 0 mg   *Fiber: 4 g*   *Sugars: 5 g*
Sugar Alcohol: 5 g

Food Exchanges: 2½ fat, 1 other carb, ½ bread

■ ■ ■

Divine Creamy Peanut Pie
Net Carbs: 13 g

1 (8 ounce) package reduced-fat cream cheese (Neufchatel)
1 cup Smuckers® natural creamy peanut butter
½ cup Splenda® sugar substitute
1 (8 ounce) carton lite frozen whipped topping, thawed

1. In mixing bowl, beat cream cheese until smooth. Add peanut butter and mix well.

2. Add sugar substitute and whipped topping and mix.

3. Spoon filling into 1 (6 ounce) graham cracker crust and refrigerate.

Optional: Garnish with Smuckers® Sugar-Free Hot Fudge Topping™.

Yield: 8 servings (1 pie)   *Serving size: ⅛ pie*

Calories (without crust): 346   *Protein: 11 g*   *Carbohydrate: 15 g*
Fat: 26 g   *Cholesterol: 21 mg*   *Sodium: 232 mg*
Calcium: 21 mg   *Fiber: 2 g*   *Sugars: 4 g*
Sugar Alcohol: 0 g

Food Exchanges: 5 fat, 1 other carb

◆

Natural peanut butter is made without sugar or hydrogenated oils and has a thicker texture than regular peanut butter.

⧉ Dreamy Pineapple Pie
Net Carbs: 31 g

1 (1 ounce) package sugar-free instant vanilla pudding mix
1 (15¾ ounce) can crushed pineapple with juice
1 (12 ounce) carton lite frozen whipped topping, thawed, divided
1 (6 ounce) reduced-fat graham cracker crust

1. In mixing bowl, combine pudding mix and pineapple with juice.

2. Fold in 1 cup whipped topping at a time and lightly mix. Pour mixture into graham cracker crust. Refrigerate until pudding sets.

Yield: 8 servings   *Serving size: ⅛ of pie*

Calories: 196	*Protein: less than 1 g*	*Carbohydrate: 31 g*
Fat: 7 g	*Cholesterol: 0 mg*	*Sodium: 236 mg*
Calcium: 0 mg	*Fiber: less than 1 g*	*Sugars: 16 g*
Sugar Alcohol: 0 g		

Food Exchanges: 1 bread, 1 fruit, 1½ fat

■ ■ ■

Cherry Coke Float
Net Carbs: 2 g

Summertime Delight!

½ to ¾ cup low-carb vanilla ice cream
1 (12 ounce) can diet cherry cola
¼ teaspoon almond extract
1 maraschino cherry with stem

1. Into tall glass, place 1 scoop ice cream and fill glass slowly with cola. Gently stir in almond flavoring. Garnish with cherry and serve immediately.

Yield: 1 serving

Calories: 100	*Protein: 2 g*	*Carbohydrate: 10 g*
Fat: 6 g	*Cholesterol: 25 mg*	*Sodium: 67 mg*
Calcium: 0 mg	*Fiber: 4 g*	*Sugars: 2 g*
Sugar Alcohol: 4 g		

Food Exchanges: 1 fat, ½ other carb

■ ■ ■

Frosty Fruit Freeze

Net Carbs: 5 g

Children and adults will love this refreshing dessert!

2 cups low-fat or fat-free buttermilk
½ cup Splenda® sugar substitute
Grated peel from 1 lemon
2 cups fresh fruit (strawberries, peaches, nectarines, blueberries, raspberries), cut in small pieces, reserving several pieces for garnish.

1. In 12-cup muffin pan, place paper muffin cups.

2. In mixing bowl, combine buttermilk, sugar substitute and grated lemon peel. Fold in fruit.

3. Spoon into muffin cups, placing reserved fruit pieces on top. Cover and freeze several hours or overnight.

4. Soften slightly at room temperature and peel off paper cups before serving.

Yield: 12 servings   *Serving size: 1 muffin cup (about ½ cup)*

Calories: 24   *Protein: 2 g*   *Carbohydrate: 5 g*
Fat: less than 1 g   *Cholesterol: 2 mg*   *Sodium: 43 mg*
Calcium: 52 mg   *Fiber: less than 1 g*   *Sugars: 3 g*
Sugar Alcohol: 0 g

Food Exchanges: 0

■ ■ ■

Bananas Foster
Net Carbs: 15 g

3 ripe bananas, peeled
½ cup fresh orange juice plus 4 tablespoons grated orange peel
3 tablespoons light butter
½ cup brown sugar substitute

1. Halve bananas lengthwise and brush with orange juice to prevent browning.

2. In large skillet over low heat, melt light butter and stir in brown sugar substitute.

3. Add bananas and remaining orange juice and cook over medium heat about 3 minutes or bananas are almost tender.

4. Sprinkle with grated orange peel.

Optional: Serve with low carb ice cream.

Yield: 6 servings   *Serving size: ½ banana*

Calories: 91   *Protein: 1 g*   *Carbohydrate: 17 g*
Fat: 3 g   *Cholesterol: 10 mg*   *Sodium: 46 mg*
Calcium: 12 mg   *Fiber: 2 g*   *Sugars: 8 g*
Sugar Alcohol: 0 g

Food Exchanges: ½ fat, 1 fruit

■ ■ ■

Chocolate-Pecan Quesadillas

Net Carbs: 3 g

4 (6 inch) low-carb tortillas
4 tablespoons reduced-fat cream cheese (Neufchatel)
2 tablespoons sugar-free hot fudge topping
2 tablespoons chopped pecans

1. Spray 2 tortillas with non-stick cooking spray.

2. On plate, place tortillas sprayed side down and spread each with 2 tablespoons cream cheese.

3. Spread 1 tablespoon fudge topping over cream cheese and sprinkle 1 tablespoon chopped pecans on top.

4. Preheat griddle or skillet on medium heat. Place one tortilla sprayed side down in skillet. Cover with another tortilla and spray with nonstick cooking spray.

5. Heat 2 minutes on each side or until browned spots appear on bottom. Remove and keep warm while second quesadilla is prepared.

6. Cut quesadillas into 8 wedges and serve immediately.

Yield: 16 servings   *Serving size: 1 wedge*

Calories: 41   *Protein: 1 g*   *Carbohydrate: 5 g*
Fat: 2 g   *Cholesterol: 3 mg*   *Sodium: 71 mg*
Calcium: 3 mg   *Fiber: 2 mg*   *Sugars: less than 1 g*
Sugar Alcohol: less than 1 g

Food Exchanges: ½ bread, ½ fat

■ ■ ■

Creamy Fruit Dream
Net Carbs: 12 g

1 (8 ounce) package reduced-fat cream cheese (Neufchatel)
1 (15 ounce) can chunky mixed fruit or fruit cocktail in juice
1 cup Splenda® sugar substitute
1 (12 ounce) carton frozen whipped topping, thawed

1. Drain fruit cocktail and reserve juice.

2. In mixing bowl, beat cream cheese and juice. Stir in whipped topping and fold in sugar substitute and fruit. Chill before serving.

Optional: Sprinkle each serving with toasted slivered almonds.

Yield: 8 to 10 servings   *Serving size: ½ cup*

Calories: 129   *Protein: 3 g*   *Carbohydrate: 13 g*
Fat: 8 g   *Cholesterol: 19 mg*   *Sodium: 107 mg*
Calcium: 19 mg   *Fiber: 1 g*   *Sugars: 8 g*
Sugar Alcohol: 0 g

Food Exchanges: 1½ fat, 1 fruit

■ ■ ■

Key Lime Pie

Net Carbs: 24 g

2 (6 ounce) cartons fat-free, no-sugar-added key lime pie yogurt
1 (3 ounce) package sugar-free lime gelatin mix
1 (8 ounce) carton lite frozen whipped topping, thawed
1 (9 inch) reduced-fat graham cracker crust

1. In mixing bowl, combine yogurt and lime gelatin and mix well.

2. Fold in whipped topping and spread mixture in pie crust.

3. Freeze.

4. Remove from freezer 20 minutes before slicing.

Yield: 8 servings   *Serving size: 1 slice*

Calories: 198   *Protein: 3 g*   *Carbohydrate: 24 g*
Fat: 8 g   *Cholesterol: 1 mg*   *Sodium: 183 mg*
Calcium: 0 mg   *Fiber: less than 1 g*   *Sugars: 11 g*
Sugar Alcohol: 0 g

Food Exchanges: 1½ bread, 1½ fat

■ ■ ■

Grapes Fantastic
Net Carbs: 16 g

⅓ cup light sour cream
¼ cup whipped cream cheese spread with cinnamon and brown
    sugar
3 cups seedless grapes, washed, drained
⅓ cup toasted slivered almonds

1. In mixing bowl, combine sour cream and cream cheese spread and mix well.

2. In separate bowl, fold cream cheese mixture into grapes until grapes are well coated. Chill 2 hours.

3. Spoon grapes into dessert bowls and sprinkle with toasted almonds.

Yield: 6 servings   *Serving size: ½ cup*

Calories: 139   *Protein: 3 g*   *Carbohydrate: 18 g*
Fat: 7 g   *Cholesterol: 11 mg*   *Sodium: 29 mg*
Calcium: 53 mg   *Fiber: 2 g*   *Sugars: 14 g*
Sugar Alcohol: 0 g

Food Exchanges: 1½ fat, 1 fruit

■ ■ ■

To Order **The Easy 4 Ingredient Diabetic Cookbook**:

Please send_____copies @ $19.95 (U.S.) each $_____

Texas residents add sales tax @ $1.60 each $_____

Plus postage/handling @ $6.00(1st copy) each $_____

$1.00 (each additional copy) $_____

Check or Credit Card (Canada-credit card only) **Total** $_____

Charge to my ☐ MasterCard. or ☐ VISA

Account #_____

Expiration Date_____

Signature_____

Mail or Call:
Cookbook Resources
541 Doubletree Dr.
Highland Village, Texas 75077
Toll Free (866) 229-2665
(972) 317-6404 Fax

Name_____

Address_____

City_____State_____Zip_____

Phone (day)_____(evening)_____

- -

To Order **The Easy 4 Ingredient Diabetic Cookbook**:

Please send_____copies @ $19.95 (U.S.) each $_____

Texas residents add sales tax @ $1.60 each $_____

Plus postage/handling @ $6.00(1st copy) each $_____

$1.00 (each additional copy) $_____

Check or Credit Card (Canada-credit card only) **Total** $_____

Charge to my ☐ MasterCard. or ☐ VISA

Account #_____

Expiration Date_____

Signature_____

Mail or Call:
Cookbook Resources
541 Doubletree Dr.
Highland Village, Texas 75077
Toll Free (866) 229-2665
(972) 317-6404 Fax

Name_____

Address_____

City_____State_____Zip_____

Phone (day)_____(evening)_____